Dear Christin,
    Congratulati_____
enjoy this book as much as we
have. We met Teri over spring
break when we went to Wichita
to visit my family. Her Mother,
Lorna, is my sister's best friend.
She is a beautiful girl and has
a wonderful testimony. We hope
you'll share it with others as
you travel through life. I know
the Lord will show you each
time someone is to read it.
    God bless you always,

        In His love,
            Judy and Bill
                Bauer

REACHING FOR THE CROWN

**A Former Beauty Queen
Travels Through A Personal Journey
Of Suffering And Faith**

Teri K. Messner

ISBN 0-9643362-0-0

First Edition
First Printing April 1995

Printed in the United States of America
Donlevy Lithograph
          Wichita, KS

Published by New Wings
Wichita, Kansas

1 2 3 4 5 6 7 8 9 — 00 99 98 97 96 95

Forward

*T*eri Messner, a former Miss Indiana of the Miss America pageant, once believed that her life was to be "crowned" with blessings from God. Her perspective changed dramatically when she was forced to face her grave while undergoing two radical brain surgeries while God remained silent. ***Reaching for the Crown*** speaks to the innermost soul of hurting people. What is your deepest pain or insecurity? Have you ever wanted to wrestle with God but been afraid to do it alone? Have you ever asked, "Where are you God?" If you have suffered in any area of life — emotionally, physically, mentally, or spiritually — then you must read this timely book. There are very few book available today for those who have endured suffering and cannot settle for easy answers. Teri's powerful message offers a letter of hope by one who has survived grave adversity. Every person should read this compassionate and inspiring new book!

— Dr. Robert H. Schuller

Introduction

My goal in writing this book is not to tell you my story, but to echo many of the experiences you may have encountered during your life and to encourage you to use your most painful circumstances as a tool to bring you greater self-esteem, with the understanding that you already know what it means to have faith. For you who have had to endure the struggles and heartaches of life are the heroes, the champions of faith. Although we all have our own individual heartaches, there is an element of understanding and camaraderie among those who must endure. I believe that the practical reality of suffering and surviving can only truly be seen from the perspective of the victims or those rare individuals who are profoundly sympathetic with those victims. When I speak on the subject of suffering, I do not merely speak from hearsay, but have had my full share of experience on the subject. Because of this, I approach the topic as honestly as possible. I will never resort to using well worn shibboleths or simplistic answers. I respect those of you who are searching too much to ask you to settle for such elementary solutions. I believe that faith must always be defined from the position of the endurer rather than from that of the idealist. I invite you to wrestle with me through some of life's most difficult moments and questions. I offer you my own experience, rather than a simple theory of how a good can be created from the most intense, undeserved suffering. Throughout the book, we will work together to help you find meaning in life and to help you make diamonds from the dust in your life.

Note:

I believe in the equality of all people, regardless of race, nationality, abilities or disabilities, and regardless of gender. Although I refer to God as "He" throughout the book, it is not my intention to genderize God, for I believe that both the male and femaleness of humanity represent the deity of God.

v

Table of Contents

Acknowledgments

To my husband Stan, my teammate in life and best friend.

To my sister Kim, my theological, philosophical fencing partner.

To my daughter Brynne, because...

To my parents Jon and Lorna Kardatzke for giving me a firm foundation on which to build.

To my other parents Arly and Marilyn Messner for their love, consistency, and friendship.

To Bruce Woods, my mentor and friend.

To Chris Kettler, a theological Tarzan.

To Marie Riggs, who brings cups of cold water to thirsty people.

To Mark Spitz and John Tobin for their compassion and creative approach to medicine.

To "Ike" Eichenberger for his interest in helping others pursue their heart-felt ministries.

In memory of Richard Merriman, who lived and died with courage.

In memory of Karen Smith who lived creatively and died courageously.

To Lucy Rogers, who turns stumbling blocks into stepping stones.

To Judy Merriman, Randy Storms, Tresa Standrich, Helen Robson, Dianne Shantz, Rick Clarke, Berny Berquist, Maxine Jack, Suzi Kardatzke, Felicia, Anne-Marie and Charlie Smith, Cathy Bouska, Pam Smith, Bobbi Hall, and Karen Smith who have chosen to be Victors instead of Victims.

In memory of Kenny Jack and Maurice "Berk" Berquist.

To Tina Markham, Lorna Johnson, Karen Finkeldei, Greta Domenic, Tracie Jordan, Dick and Wilda Young, Jim and Linda Snook, Gail Johnson, Millie Ellison, Bonnie Parker, Jack and Joyce Cassell, because of the people they are.

To Debi Johnson for her loyal friendship and to "Louise" for her excellent business sense.

To George Gardner who dares to live soulfully with integrity.

In appreciation to Mike Noller who works to prepare people for the future.

Special thanks to Lorna Kardatzke, Kathy Smith and Juanita Royer for editorial assistance.

In memory of Keith Gray, I understand now.

In appreciation to the Miss America organization for making it possible for young women to obtain a platform from which to speak.

AND THE WINNER IS ...

CHAPTER I

*I do not want to die until I have
faithfully made the most of my talent and
cultivated the seed that was placed in me until
the last small twig has grown.*
Kathe Kollwitz

And The Winner Is ...

"I know what I'm going to be when I grow up Mommy," a skinny little seven-year-old girl confidently declared one crisp fall evening in the living room of her home.

"Oh, really?" An unimpressed mother answered mechanically.

"Yes, I'm going to be Miss America!"

The seven-year-old girl was none other than myself, expressing a desire that most American little girls feel is their destiny while watching all the beauties parade in the Miss America pageant every year.

"There she is, Miss America..." Bert Parks belted out the traditional song as a new beauty was crowned.

"That's going to be me someday, Mother," I whispered, as I watched in awe and wishful admiration.

My mother, like most mothers, took my declaration with a grain of salt. My father, however, thought it wasn't a bad idea. Over the years I went from piano lessons to voice lessons to poise classes in order to be able to step into the role I was "predestined" for.

At seventeen I was old enough to enter a Miss America preliminary. I won the local title and thought I was on my way to fulfilling my purpose for being alive. My dreams were dashed when my name was called too soon at the state pageant. I was runner-up and the winner of the swimsuit award, not the queen.

"You're just too young," I was told. "Your time will come. Get some schooling behind you and you'll win next year."

I was told that academics were extremely important so I maintained an "A" average while learning how to pivot turn. At nineteen, I entered again, captured the local title and then went on to compete at the state level.

Three hundred thousand women, all over the nation, compete every year in the hope that they will be one of the final fifty who will walk down the glamorous Miss America runway while the entire country watches. My hopes were high as I went into the final night of competition. I had won the preliminary talent award. It seemed that all was in my favor. Finally, when the competition was completed, the host of the pageant declared that it was time to crown the new queen. The top ten finalists were asked to return to the stage for the announcement.

The out-going Miss Indiana had taken her place on center stage and was holding the beautiful rhinestone crown that every little girl dreams of wearing as an impressive list of prizes was announced. The new Miss Indiana would be guaranteed a year's contract of paid appearances throughout the state of Indiana as well as an all expenses paid trip to compete in the Miss America pageant. She would receive a two thousand dollar scholarship to the university of her choice and would travel to Haiti as a special guest of the ambassador of Haiti, who was one of the judges that night. The new beauty queen would also be the proud owner of a brand new car that would have her name and the Miss Indiana title engraved on both sides of the automobile.

The tension was mounting. The fourth runner-up was announced, then the third, the second, the first, and finally came the familiar words:

"AND THE WINNER IS ..."

The Master of Ceremonies paused dramatically to increase our anticipation as a drum roll began to help intensify the moment ... finally ... *"The new Miss Indiana is contestant number 14, Miss Anderson, Teri Kardatzke."* I took my place, center stage. A lovely rhinestone crown was pinned to the top of my head, and a shining set of car keys was placed in my hand. As I took the traditional walk down the runway, I thought, *"Life is falling into place, just as I have planned."*

Little did I know that soon after that magical moment, a dreadful event would take place that would resurface years later to tragically affect my life forever. Had I known what was in store for me, I would have turned around that very instant, handed back the glittering crown and the car keys and said, *"Thanks, but no thanks!"*

Of course, none of us can peer into the future, so I waltzed into my new role as "Miss Indiana" with eager anticipation. Part of my new job included preparing to compete in the Miss America pageant and making public appearances throughout the state. My first appearance was at a glamorous county fair. I was to sign autographs in the "major event" tent right next to the "prized pig" trough. There was a thin partition separating the pigs from me. Suddenly, from the other side of the partition, I heard the voice of a man with a strong, slow midwestern drawl say:

"Honey, I just met Miss Indiana!"

"Oh really, what does she look like?" A woman's voice answered.

"Well—she's skinny— with a paint job!" Was his descriptive reply.

Shortly following this noteworthy happening, I was rushed to Indianapolis to ride in the "Indianapolis 500" parade. My partner in the car was none other than Dan Quayle, who at that time was an Indiana Senator. The following day I returned to my home town of Anderson, Indiana, to pack for the next event that I was scheduled to attend that evening.

At twelve o'clock noon, I loaded my official "Miss Indiana" car and drove to the first stop light past my home. The light turned red just as I got there. I glanced into my rear view mirror and saw a semi-trailer truck coming toward me. I quickly realized the driver wasn't slowing down. I remember thinking frantically, *"He's not going to stop! He's not going to stop!"*

5

He didn't ...

I felt a horrible jolt and heard a disastrous crash. The next thing I knew, I was in the hospital with a knot on the right side of my head. It was determined later that at the time of the crash, the driver of the semi-truck was going sixty miles an hour. The beautiful car I had won was demolished. The doctor informed me that I had received a slight concussion and whiplash. He told me I would heal quickly and I did ...

... so we *thought.*

The next day a picture of my poor car was on the front page of the newspaper and my neck hurt. Other than that, there was nothing left of the accident but a haunting memory ... *I assumed.* Who would have ever guessed that a few years later the haunting memory would surface into a nightmare reality of physical torment and anguish? Time would painfully reveal that the accident was the primary event that would cause me to experience an individual holocaust in a concentration camp of suffering.

The memory of the collision began to fade as the Miss America pageant loomed ahead. For the event, I had adopted the scripture:

> *"In everything you do put God first and he will direct you and crown your efforts with success"*
> (Proverbs 3:5)
> Living Bible

At the time, in my theological *naiveté*, I interpreted this scripture to mean that God would reward me with the Miss America title because I was a Christian. The scripture says "crown," right!(?) I imagined touring around the country wearing the Miss America crown, speaking to hundreds of thousands of eager listeners, telling members of each audience to *"put God first and He will crown*

6

your efforts." I hoped this was God's will. I was a Christian, right? I'd bargain each time I prayed:

"If you will allow me to win, God, I'll tour for you. Just think of all the people I could reach, God! I'll do it for you!"

It made perfect sense to me. What a life I had dreamed up! What a lie.

The big week arrived. My lovely sequined gowns were safely packed. My mind was full of expectations and anticipation. It was God's will, right? Upon arrival in Atlantic City, I discovered that God had "told" several other hopefuls the same thing! The week was a mixture of glamour and stress. Part of the glamour included meeting celebrities such as Ron Ely, alias Tarzan, who was the host of the pageant.

We state winners smiled our best pageant smiles all week long, continuously putting Vaseline on our teeth so that our lips would not stick to them. One never knew when a reporter would snap an unexpected photograph. On one occasion I was photographed while I was singing into a spoon. When clowning around backstage, I used a large mixing spoon as a microphone to rehearse my talent number. The picture ended up on the front page of my hometown news!

Rehearsals for the talent competition began. I soon realized that talent was abundant among my competitors. The television presentation does not do these lovely ladies justice. The public rarely sees all the talent that is prevalent among the fifty representatives.

Evening gown rehearsals began. The elegant gowns were of a wide variety in selection and price. One former Miss America had won in a second-hand gown she had bought at a garage sale for $50.00. One of my competitors paraded in a gown bearing a $30,000.00 price tag that had been loaned to her state pageant.

Oddly enough, the naked eye couldn't tell the difference between the two as far as glitter and glamour were concerned.

The swimsuit competition was next. Back stage, girls were padding and taping "natural" all-American figures into place. The stage was full of physically fit women. Competition was tough. While I was on stage, with thousands of people staring at my legs, I kept thinking to myself, *"I should have lifted more weights or given up that extra chocolate after all."*

Saturday evening finally arrived. The new "Miss America" was crowned and the traditional *"There She Is"* was sung, but not to me. The rest of us who represented the *"There She Wasn't"* population, returned home to reign over our individual states. I spent the remainder of my reign performing such important duties as cutting ribbons and riding in parades with such notables as the country music star J. C. Riley, Lyle Wagner from the Carol Burnett Show, and Dick Van Dyke's lovable sidekick—Morey Amsterdam. (Don't you just hate it when people name-drop? Sandi Patti and I were talking about that just the other day! She and Billy Graham had discussed it earlier that week!)

Two events of that year stand out in my mind. Purdue University asked me to appear for them at the annual basketball game between the two big rivals, the hosting Purdue Boilermakers and the Indiana University Hoosiers. When I walked to the center of that packed stadium, I was crushed to hear the Purdue fans booing loudly. It seems that I had unwittingly worn a red dress and red is I.U.'s color. The Purdue fans had understandably greeted me as the enemy, while the visiting I.U. fans cheered wildly. Following basketball had never been one of my hobbies and I felt like crawling under the bleachers. (Incidentally, I was never asked back!)

The other event took place in Indianapolis the day before the Indy 500. One of the cute, young drivers had caught my eye, and as I intently tried to steal glances at him throughout the autograph signing party an older gentleman attempted to strike up a conversation with me. I was too intent on trying to capture the undivided attention of the cute driver to pay any attention to the man who wouldn't quit bothering me. I knew he looked relatively familiar, but it wasn't until he had walked away that I realized I had been ignoring Bob Barker from the TV show "The Price is Right!"

I spent much of the remaining part of the year speaking at various functions, wearing my rhinestone crown, and quoting Proverbs 3:4-5. Then an event took place that introduced me to a world of undeserved suffering, altered my perspective on my year of glamour and, at a preliminary level, caused me to question the blessing-dumping god I had grown up believing in.

I was invited to a hospital in Chicago to meet patients and to sign autographs. On that particular day the hospital staff was giving a birthday party for a terminally ill child. I was invited to attend. As I walked into the party room, my eyes immediately fell on a beautiful girl with long blonde curls. She was about thirteen or fourteen and had been born without arms or legs. I walked over to her to get acquainted. The first thing she said was:

"See my necklace? Can I call you Mommy?"

Puzzled, I looked at the nurse beside her. She took my arm and led me out of ear shot and explained, "Debbi's parents abandoned her the day she was born. Her home has always been here. No one visits her. No one outside the hospital staff seems to care about her. The necklace she wears was given to her by her best friend, a little girl who died of leukemia last year. She never wants it off and talks about it constantly."

Our attention then turned to another little girl with big brown eyes. It was her birthday celebration. The hospital staff informed me that this might be her last birthday for she also had been diagnosed with leukemia and was in the last stages of the disease. She blew out her candles and began to open a large pile of presents that her family and the staff had given her. Her smile was brilliant and as she continued to unwrap her presents I glanced back at Debbie.

All I could see was loneliness and sadness in her eyes as she watched the festivities from a distance. I continued to watch her out of the corner of my eye throughout the party. Thirty minutes had passed and Debbie had not uttered a word. Then suddenly, she called out, "Janet, come here. I have something for you."

The birthday girl put down the beautifully wrapped present she was about to open and was wheeled over to Debbie. Debbie looked up at her attending nurse and in a small, timid voice said, "Please take off my necklace."

Silence fell over the entire room. After a thoughtful pause Janet protested, "But it's *your* necklace!"

"Not anymore," Debbie stated simply. "Happy Birthday."

As the nurse transferred the tiny necklace from one child to the other, Debbie's face beamed with the joy of giving all she had to another. The rest of us were wiping away tears of disbelief. Still captured by the beauty of the moment, Debbie caught me by surprise when she broke the silence, turned to me and said, "It must be wonderful to be you. You are somebody special. I wish I was you."

How could I begin to explain to this precious child that what I had just witnessed her doing was more important than anything that I had ever done in my life? I asked myself, as I stood beside her with a rhinestone crown glittering on my head, which one of us had truly captured the essence of life? Which one of us deserved to be wearing a crown? Which one of us really understood what love and faith is? I had actually asked God to be crowned "Miss America." This lovely child, who didn't have her arms or legs, simply shared what she had with another who had less. In a brief moment, she demonstrated to me that somewhere along the way I had missed what life was all about. I began to realize that though the crown on my head sparkled brilliantly and had promised a fantasy life full of glamour, it was empty inside. Without recognizing it, I believe that Debbie was wearing an invisible crown of unselfishness and humility. Had we been able to see it, it would have sparkled so brilliantly that we would not have been able to comprehend its beauty.

My heart ached with emptiness for the remainder of my reigning year. Then the time arrived to crown a new "Miss." While taking my final walk down the glittering runway I remember feeling relieved that the year had come to a close. Debbie's gesture had left quite an impression. Before that year, I thought that I would attain happiness and purpose once I had won a rhinestone crown. By the end of the year, I realized how dull my crown was in comparison to the joy that had radiated from Debbie's face, as she gave all she had to another who had less. I was anxious to get on with life, to find a new challenge.

The following year I moved to Wichita, Kansas, to complete my college education, majoring in speech and drama with a minor in opera. I graduated with honors. In the middle of my senior year I met my husband-to-be and within a year we were married.

Life was busy over the next six years. During that time, my husband earned his doctorate in medicine, set up a private practice, and our daughter Brynne Marie was born.

I still had stars in my eyes during all this time, believing that I would find fulfillment in the world of entertainment. I sang in a variety of events, varying from Bob Hope tours to "The Miss USA" pageant, and began a career as a television host. I was still in search of purpose for my life and believed that the exciting world of television held the answer.

One of the programs I hosted was a Saturday night state-wide game show with a big wheel on the set that six contestants would spin for prizes. It was my role as the hostess to say, *"SPIN THE WHEEL!"* Even with that "meaningful" job, I still felt empty inside. Imagine that!

THE FAIRY TALE ENDS

CHAPTER II

Adversity is the first path to truth.
Lord Byron

The Fairy Tale Ends

The first time it happened was on a beautiful spring day as I was taking my usual early morning two-mile jog. I was an avid jogger in great physical shape, with no history whatsoever of any type of chronic illness. My family life was secure, and the television show I hosted was successful. I was twenty-seven years old and I had the world by the tail! How could I have possibly known that what would happen in the next instant would soon change my barbie doll existence into a prison of despair?

Suddenly, as I was jogging around a bend in the road, I experienced the strangest *dejá vu* type sensation I had ever known. I remember thinking to myself, *"How strange. What on earth was that?"* Without thinking much more about it, I completed my jog, not realizing that the little sensation was an indication of something that would change my life forever. It was, simply, the shower before the storm.

A week after this seemingly insignificant experience, I began to wake up with excruciating headaches every morning. Jogging would relieve the headaches for about twenty minutes, then they would return to stay with me all day. I started having several of these *dejá vu* sensations every week, sometimes several a day. I began to call them "spells." I understandably became concerned and began to look for doctors with answers. A large variety of tests were run over the next three years, from CT scans to EEGs. I went to eight different neurologists and received eight different diagnoses, from "panic attacks" to possible tumors. One physician even told me that the fillings in my teeth were causing trauma to my brain and that my jaw was out of line.

Meanwhile, the "spells" were increasing in intensity and frequency. Immediately following the *dejá vu* experience, I would "blank out" and not know where I was or who I was. The "spells" would leave me completely exhausted, and frequently the pressure in my head was so intense that I could do nothing but sleep constantly. Even sleep could not relieve the pressure, and I would wake up as exhausted as I had been before I had gone to sleep. By the end of the second year I was having, on the average, twenty-one "spells" a month and needing to sleep nineteen hours a day. I suddenly found myself completely disabled, unable even to take care of our young daughter. Life had become a nightmare of pain. Almost overnight, my fantasy fairytale existence had reversed into a tragic, lamentable reality. Still, there were no answers.

Finally, we found a wonderful doctor with a valid explanation to my frustrating, life-altering dilemma. Mark Spitz, MD (the doctor, not the swimmer!) of University Hospital in Denver, Colorado, was the man who began the process toward finding a solution. He was kind and compassionate and he spent well over an hour listening to my story, going over the previous records of all the tests I had taken and examining me.

At the end of the examination, he said, "Ms. Messner, I believe I know what is going on with you. I believe you have Adult-Onset Epilepsy of the right temporal lobe in your brain."

It took a moment for me to absorb the reality of his diagnosis. At first, I felt relieved that I had finally been given a reasonable answer. Then the actuality of the fact that I had somehow developed an illness I knew virtually nothing about brought forth a flood of questions. *Epilepsy?... Me?... Why?... How?...* I was a young adult woman who had been healthy all of my life. I was an achiever, a wife, a mother, a former beauty queen. I had graduated from college with honors. I had a successful television career. *Epilepsy? Me?* How could this have happened? What did this mean for my future? I had naively believed that I was in control of my life. I had planned my entire life and dealing with an unexpected physical illness had never been included in my agenda.

"How could this have happened?" I asked Dr. Spitz.

"Epilepsy can develop in any person at any time," he explained. "The disorder can surface for a wide variety of reasons, such as the result of suffering a stroke, heredity, or any head injury such as a blow suffered in an automobile accident…"

The traumatic memory of the car wreck surfaced in my mind. Once again, I could recall the sound of the crash and the jolt of the impact. Was it possible that the injury from my Miss Indiana days could have caused this? (I discovered later that sometimes epilepsy will not surface for several years after a blow to the head, although not every head injury results in seizures.)

As I allowed the frightening news to sink in, I realized that I was not certain what epilepsy was. I asked Dr. Spitz to explain:

"It might surprise you to know that epilepsy is fairly common. In fact, it's as common as diabetes, but you rarely will hear anyone talking about it. Although **two million Americans** have to endure living with recurring seizures, (epilepsy) of some type, and approximately **twenty-five million Americans** have actually experienced having a seizure in their lifetime, seizures and epilepsy are still very misunderstood by the general population. There is a myth that people with epilepsy are unintelligent. That is pure nonsense. Many people who have had to endure this health problem have been known to have high IQs, including:

- James Madison, fifth president of the United States,
- Mozart and Paganini, the brilliant composers,
- Charles Dickens, British author of *A Christmas Carol,*
- Socrates, the philosopher,
- Alexander the Great, the great conqueror,
- Joan of Arc, the famous crusader,
- Vincent Van Gogh, the Dutch artist,
- Napoleon Bonaparte, the French dictator,
- Fyodor Dostoyevsky, author of *Crime and Punishment,*
- Grover Cleveland Alexander, the major league baseball pitcher,

17

- and NBA basketball all-star Bobby Jones.
- Other famous people from history include St. Paul of the Bible, Peter the Great, Alfred Tennyson, and Alfred Nobel. You're in great company!"

While the information was comforting and surprising, I still was not confident in my understanding of what epilepsy actually was, so I asked Dr. Spitz to elaborate.

"To explain epilepsy, I like to use an analogy. Let's compare the brain to a Civic Center in your community where concerts are held.

Civic Center

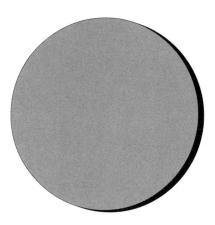

"Let's imagine, that in this Civic Center, there are two concert halls. In Concert Hall I, which is the largest concert hall, the symphony is always playing. The audience is relaxed and thus able to absorb the music of the great masters.

"In the smaller concert hall, Concert Hall II, there is always a *ROCK CONCERT* going on! Because the music in Concert Hall II is noisy and irritating, the audience members are excitable, volatile, and easily stirred into violence.

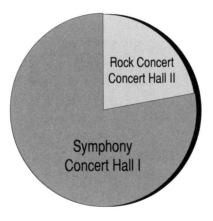

"Each audience member in the concert hall represents a cell in your brain. The brain cells in Concert Hall II are extremely active, overactive, just like the excitable audience members at a rock concert. Using the analogy, let's say one member of the audience in Concert Hall II shoves another member and that member shoves back. Because the audience is high strung and agitated, a riot breaks out. The audience members get out of control and the riotous crowd infiltrates through the other concert hall, disrupting the symphony.

"This is an imaginative way of describing what happens in the brain with brain cells that will result in a seizure. One or two brain cells that are overactive bump into each other, so to speak. If the cells that surround them are volatile cells, they will join in the over activity. This extra stimulus causes the brain to overwork, which causes an electrical disturbance in the brain and thus results in a seizure.

"There are many different types of seizures. When most people hear the word epilepsy, they automatically think of grand mal seizures where the whole body is involved. Actually, this is only one type of seizure. The medical term for the seizures you have been experiencing is partial-complex seizures of the right temporal lobe. We could describe it as someone turning off the lights in the concert hall for a moment or two to cause confusion among the audience members. Partial complex seizures are not very noticeable to other people, but they are the most difficult to control with medicine.

"Usually when a riot breaks out, the police are called in and tear gas is distributed. The tear gas represents medicine. In your case the rock music that is being played in Concert Hall II is HEAVY METAL, so the tear gas *(medicine)* really won't work. *(The bad news.)*

"However, we can take out the entire concert hall:

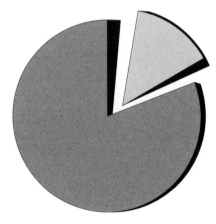

Then renovate the civic center into one concert hall where the symphony always plays." *(The **good** news?)*

21

Symphony
Concert Hall I

"Great let's do it!" I said.

"Wait a minute," he cautioned. "This is a dangerous surgery. You must be aware of the risks that are involved."

"What are they?" I asked.

"There is a possibility you could become paralyzed or lose your life."

He sent me home to think about it.

Another month went by and the seizures were coming on so frequently that my entire body was becoming depressed, and I was sleeping more than nineteen hours a day. Not only that, but the seizures were increasing in intensity. After a seizure, I would pass out in a dead faint. The pain in my head was unbearable, and I was quickly becoming disabled. The seizures were taking away my memory. I noticed that I could barely recall any events that had taken place during the last three years. The smallest tasks were becoming major mountains. I despised going to sleep because I knew I would only wake up exhausted, needing to go back to sleep. Sleep had become an enemy, and it was winning the war.

Christmas was three weeks away. My patient husband had the house beautifully decorated from top to bottom. The Yuletide season had always been my favorite time of year, and I had loved decorating our home in great anticipation. That particular year I did not have the strength to even help put the ornaments on the tree. As I lay on the couch the night the tree was decorated I was in a daze, holding my head to try to stop the pain that was constantly throbbing in my brain. Our little daughter asked questions periodically: "Mommy, won't you help? Why won't my Mommy help, Daddy? Why does my Mommy have to have spells and be sick all the time?"

"What has happened to me?" I asked myself in amazement.

Where was the young woman who had once been accused of having enough energy for ten people? Where was the vivacious, active person that I had identified myself as? I had always been a person that people accused of never sitting still for more than a moment or two. Suddenly I didn't have the strength to stay awake for more than an hour. I knew I could not live like that anymore. I was not living. I was unable to participate in life. I was only able to watch others live. Life was going on all around me and I was not able to join in.

I loved my family, but I was unable to take care of them. The illness was too great. It had become my life. I felt inadequate, useless. My life seemed to lack any purpose since I spent every day, almost every moment, sleeping. I was in horrendous pain constantly. It was embarrassing to me to feel so helpless. I couldn't see any purpose for life when I wasn't physically able to even stay awake, and when I was awake I was in constant pain. Life was over, I thought. I wanted to die. God seemed far away. I remember asking Him repeatedly, *"Where are you?"*

Nothing would answer...

"I can't serve you like this. Why are you allowing this to happen? I have work to do," I reminded God.

Nothing answered ...

"If you don't need me then just let me die."

Nothing ...

The Nothing became my close companion.[1] I would pray, Nothing would answer. We became good friends. In desperation I

23

cried, *"What do you want me to do, God?"* The Nothing replied. *"Are you there, God? Do you care that I am facing the worst time of my life? Do you care that I feel alone? Do you care that I'm frightened? Do you care that I'm in constant pain?"* Nothing. *"Why did you allow this to happen? What could I have possibly done to deserve this?"* Only the Nothing responded. Day after torturous, pain-filled day, this pattern continued. As the days turned into month after dreadful month, I knew I was going to have to make a choice to either become bitter toward a silent God or to accept the nothingness as God's way of communicating with me. Since the Nothing had become my constant comrade, I decided I might as well become friends with it.

The Nothing taught me many things over the next few months.[2] It slowly taught me that the theology that I had been exposed to in a traditional American Christian home and then had adopted for my own, was not sufficient for a person going through an extreme trauma. If it was not sufficient for the painful times of life, then it would not be adequate for the ordinary days either. If the "truths" that I had believed in didn't hold true under extreme distress, then they were not really truths. Where was the god that crowned beauty queens who prayed to him regularly? Where was the god who rewarded the faithful with rhinestones? That god had failed me. Was there any other?

Throughout the next few months I began to understand that although the god of the American Sunday school classroom sustains a person day to day in relatively ordinary situations, it doesn't hold many answers for real life trauma. The god of the Sunday school classroom doesn't seem to take into account the purpose of living in an unfair world where pain and suffering are prevalent.

Why, for example, would a loving God answer the prayers of a girl who pleads to be "Miss America" and yet allow an innocent orphan in a cold hospital to face life every day without any limbs or anyone to love her? Why does God allow little children in

Somalia to die of starvation without intervening? Why would a loving God answer the prayer of the American Everyman who prays for a good parking space on a Sunday morning and yet allow the concentration camp victim to suffer unspeakable torture at the hands of a Nazi soldier? This almighty Santa Claus, this prayer-answering god that I had grown up believing in was too inconsistent to be credible.

As an evangelical, typical church-attending believer, I had always thought, somehow, that I was someone special, that God would be there to answer my needs whenever I would call on Him. I believed that He would shelter me from harm so that I could perform whatever special task God had planned *just for me* to do. Instead, I found myself quickly disillusioned when this god whom I had believed would always comfort and protect me, was ignoring me, seemingly oblivious to my anguish. Where was this loving God, this almighty parent, whom I had been raised to believe in? Did He care at all? Why was He silent? Who was the God I was beginning to get to know that allows so much pain and suffering in this world of ours? As I became one of those who has been hurt by life, the suffering of all humanity became increasingly important to me. Where could I begin to search for answers?

When I found traditional faith too sanguine to sustain me through the dark hours, I began a long, difficult search for universal truths. If God were not the god I had learned about in the traditional American church, then who was He? How could I begin to find Him? The promising, encouraging god of Sunday school was nowhere to be found. In his place was the experience of the Nothing.[3]

I decided it was time to do some serious research to try to find the God who is and to let go of the illusions of the god I wanted him to be. The God who is seems to leave creation alone at times of horrendous suffering. Why? Who is this God? Surely, I was not the only person who had met the silent God during a time of crisis. Slowly, I began collecting reports of people who had also felt

25

abandoned by God during a time of unjust suffering. In the following chapter, I will introduce you to a number of people who have experienced extreme suffering and the silence of God. In other words, if you have ever felt alone, you are not alone.

SERPENTS AND STONES

CHAPTER III

Oh, isn't life a terrible thing, thank God?
Dylan Thomas

Serpents and Stones

*W*here is God when life hurts? Who is this God who doesn't seem to follow through? Where is the God of the Bible who appears to make empty promises to people?

> *"Ask, and it will be given to you; seek, and you will find;*
> *knock, and the door will be opened to you.*
> *For everyone who asks receives,*
> *and he who seeks finds, and to him who knocks it will be opened.*
> **What man is there among you who, if his son asks for bread,**
> **will give him a stone? Or if he asks for a fish,**
> **will he give him a serpent?**
> *If you then, being evil, know how to give good gifts to your children,*
> *how much more will your Father who is in heaven*
> *give good things to those who ask Him!"*
>
> (Matt. 7:8 -11, NKJ)

This scripture seems to promise that if we will just ask, knock, and seek, God will give good gifts to His children. Right? Then why do so many people in this world continue to suffer unjustly?

"I'm asking," I prayed day after day while I was in so much physical pain that I could barely even lift my head off my pillow. *"What do you want from me?"* I questioned the silent God. *"I'm seeking you. Please help me,"* I pleaded while holding my head as it throbbed in horrendous pain. The Nothing continued to be my closest companion.

Where was God? Were the assuring words in the Bible just empty promises? What does a scripture such as this possibly have to say to the faith-filled Christian who has just been told that she has to have a piece of her brain removed in order to possibly ever have a normal life again? What does a scripture like this one have to say to all of humanity who have had to face almost incomprehensible suffering or tragedy? How can a god who promises to give good gifts to His children if they only ask, seek, and knock, ever be believed in again by a person who has lived through a nightmare of suffering in which He remained silent?

Where is God when life hurts? Where is God in the personal holocaust experience? Does He care? Does He even exist at all? During my personal holocaust time I developed a feeling of camaraderie with other people who had experienced great suffering. Although the details of their pain and mine were different, a passionate empathy for anyone who had suffered or was suffering grew within me. I believe that pain transcends details. The feelings of hurt, loneliness, and abandonment are universal. All humans, at one time or another, cry out *"why me?"* to an unseen God who seems to remain silent. How can a person ever believe again in a God of love after living through a personal hell? How can the couple who has stood beside the freshly dug grave of their three-month-old only child who died in the night of sudden infant death syndrome ever believe in a God who gives good gifts again? *"Why?"* the mother cried in despair. God was silent. What about the straight "A" model student who had his spinal cord severed in a car accident that was caused by a driver who swerved over into his lane for no apparent reason, when the student was enroute to the state fair for a day of innocent fun? The driver walked away unharmed. The teenager, once the star running back on his high school football team, struggles daily to relearn how to perform such simple tasks as putting on his own socks with hands that can't move anymore. *"Why?"* the boy still cries day after pain-filled day, month after month. Throughout the entire struggle, God has remained silent.

We have all heard the stories of Holocaust victims in Nazi concentration camps who saw their entire families brutally murdered, including some who witnessed their own babies being thrown up into the air and then caught on the way down by the sharp edge of a bayonet.[4] All the while, God stayed silent. Why?

Where is the loving God of Sunday school whom we were taught to believe directs us in everyday activities, answers our prayers, helps us find the right job and choose the right mate? Where is this God who is supposed to be interested in our pain, our suffering, and our happiness and who is involved in our lives? Where is the Holy Spirit that is, according to traditional doctrine, communicating with us and comforting us in the darkest hours of life? Is there purpose for the senseless pain that is so abundant in our world? Is there really a good God who cares for His creation? Is there really a good God who answers when we ask, seek, and knock? If so, how can a God who is good remain silent and seem totally oblivious to anguish when His children are enduring unspeakable sufferings? Where is this God, this almighty parent who answers prayers and who promises to give us more than we even give our own children whom we love and treasure? Where is this God who promises to give His children more than bread and fish when they pray? *Many people seem to receive serpents and stones, instead of bread and fish.* Why? How can the individual who has survived such tragedies when God was silent possibly trust and believe in a god who cares for the remainder of his or her life?

For the first time in my life, I had to personally and soberly face the age-old problem of suffering and the silence of God. I had to rethink much of the traditional dogma that I had been raised to believe in. My Christian upbringing taught me that Christ took our place on the cross at Calvary and that somehow we are personally exempt from serpents and stones. I had also believed that if anything undesirable would happen, that somehow God would be there to comfort "His children" through the power of the Holy

31

Spirit. I was taught to view religion in black and white terms —God is good; Satan is evil— never having to take into account the gray area of good people who suffered. I was sorely equipped to face the reality of what it means to be fully human, and my voice joined in the chorus of all those who have suffered: *"Unfair! Why Me?"*

I believe part of the reason we are left unable to creatively handle suffering and pain when we are faced with it is that we have a warped idea of what it really means to be a human being. We, who call ourselves Christians, have been rightly accused of avoiding the stark realities of living in this world and hiding our faces in the sand, as an ostrich does, when life gets tough. We want to deny the reality of the existence of "serpents and stones" (pain, disappointments, God-forsakenness, and suffering) and want to claim that all God's children will receive "bread and fish" (blessings abundant) to sustain us whenever we pray as long as we believe *enough.* We are among the first to issue judgment on those who must endure and the first to resort to using empty shibboleths such as *"God revealed to me," "The spirit is leading me to...," "Pray for more faith," "God must be trying to teach you something."* These do nothing except tear away at the faith of the person who has had to live through a personal holocaust and God-forsaken experience.

They also reveal that Christians are, many times, afraid to face life realistically and that we adopt small definitions of who God is and what faith is. We do not very often escape our own personal wishes for a Santa Claus-type god who eagerly answers our every whim every time we ask, seek, and knock, in order to be able to seriously ask why so many people who have feelings, needs, and desires just as we ourselves do have to live a lifetime enduring unjust pain, suffering, and agony. For example, *Why would a loving and inclusive God help one person in suburban America find the perfect house (bread and fish type gift) while He allows hundreds and thousands upon thousands to die everyday of starvation? (serpents and stones.)*

32

How do we go about realistically facing these big picture questions and retain a belief in a loving God who cares about our individual lives? One of the goals of this book is to do just that. It's important to expand our ideas of what it means to be a human being and what it really means to have faith in a loving God in a world where individuals suffer much pain and seem to receive serpents and stones when they pray.

Instead of preparing people for the fact that a part of living in this world includes having to deal with serpents and stones at times, the organized church, which is currently being overly influenced by some people in the Charismatic movement, is mass producing us into faith robots who expect bread and fish all the time. Faith robots are Christians who narrowly think the same, believe they have a divine right to blessings abundant and share small definitions of who God is and what it means to *"have faith."* I see why many times organized religion is laughed at by individuals who are daring enough to ask inclusive questions. We are, by and large, unthinking robots, afraid of a bigger God than we can create in our own small definition of faith. We want to retain our safe definitions of a Santa Claus-type god, and we have that luxury until we, as individuals, become the ones who are suffering. We have that privilege until *"we"* who pray to Santa Claus for bread and fish gifts become *"they"* who must endure living with serpents and stones.

All of us will, most likely, at some time in our lives, be faced with a personal crisis of some sort where the Santa god won't sustain us any longer. That is why we should passionately open our minds to new possibilities and definitions of what faith really is. Faith includes accepting the reality of the existence of serpents and stones and the silence of God.

Who can possibly help us face the reality of anguish and the silence of God? Only someone who has experienced extreme suffering while God remained silent will do. I believe that the practical reality of suffering can only truly be seen from the perspective of the victims or those rare individuals who are profoundly sympathetic with those victims.[5] *Outsiders,* those who haven't personally lived through an experience of extreme suffering, should never assume an authoritative role while discussing the subject with *insiders.* Only insiders have earned that authority. What better insider to go to for disclosure than the historical, controversial Jesus of Nazareth who had experienced dreadful suffering on the cross at Golgotha?[6]   While facing the reality of serpents and stones in my own life, I decided to begin reading the account of His death to see if I could find some truths there that I could apply to my own situation.

I discovered that the historical Jesus was well acquainted with the Nothing. He knew the feeling of being alone and abandoned by God. *"My God, my God, why have you forsaken me?"* (Matt. 27:46, NKJ)[7]   An incident of Nothing answering was even experienced by the One who is called the Son of God. There it is in black and white. The Nothing is a common occurrence. Somehow, just having the knowledge that someone else had experienced Nothing answering gave me just enough comfort to feel a little less than completely alone.

The account of His cry on the cross told me that He knew abandonment and pain.[8] His cry from the position of an *insider* reveals that this is part of the journey of faith. We shouldn't be surprised when sufferings and disappointments enter our lives. We constantly rebel against the idea that we all have to deal with the consequences of living in an imperfect world that contains serpents and stones. Yet this is the reality of the journey of life.

"In the world you will have tribulation..."
(John 16:33, NKJ)

The fact is that all of humanity will continue to experience difficulties. Life is not and never will be perfect. The Nothing is a reality, but we weren't left alone to deal with the silence of God. We have been given an example in the account of the life of Jesus that shows us that to continue to believe while experiencing suffering and the silence of God is in reality faith itself.

> *"But, take courage; I have conquered the world!"*
> (John 16:33, NRSV)

The doctrine of God-forsakenness and abandonment is actually the Christian doctrine.[9] With this understanding, I slowly began to build a theology of solidarity with humanity through the experience of God-forsakenness and abandonment which includes a new definition of the word "crown."

> *"Blessed is the man who perseveres under trial;*
> *for once he has been approved he will receive the **crown** of life,*
> *which the Lord has promised to those who love Him."*
> (James 1:12,NAS)

In the naiveté of my glamorous past, I had defined "crown" as immediate prosperity. I had believed that somehow I had been chosen by God to have blessings galore and that I deserved them because, after all, I was a Christian! (The bread and fish mentality.) It was a theology full of pride, selfishness, egotism, and wishful thinking. It was the theology of Americanized Christianity sometimes known as the health/wealth, prosperity gospel. This warped gospel proclaims that we are a blessed people and a blessed nation,[10] that somehow God has chosen to heap material and earthly blessings upon us so that we can lead other "less fortunate" people to Christ. It is a gospel that exalts those the world exalts and blames the victims who seem to receive serpents and stones in this unjust world.

Our current society has created a class structure of upper, lower, and middle. We who call ourselves Christians sometimes accept this structure and in our safe, veneer Christian state whisper to ourselves:

35

"The afflicted and oppressed,
(those who seem to receive serpents and stones),
are not born inferior to us.
We love them. We realize, however, forces of circumstance have
made them inferior. (Less whole, therefore, less acceptable
to God) For God, we cry, desires blessings abundant for
His people." [11]

I knew this doctrine well. I had innocently lived and indirectly proclaimed the "crown" gospel in my beauty queen days. Suddenly, I had become one of its victims.

It is a gospel that merely reflects the world's own message back to the world. It is an easy, non-threatening creed that allows us to think that it's God's will for us to succeed with an overabundance of good fortune.[12] We have become pretentious martyrs.

"See how holy I am.
See how God has blessed my family,
my church, and myself because of our holiness.
If you were to lay down your life for God
as I have then God would heap
blessings on you, too!"

This gospel, which is alive and well in our modern day church, is not only not preparing people for real life, but is actually persecuting those who must face the painful realities of living in this imperfect world.[13] It's a faithless church that persecutes those who must endure living a pain-filled existence by proclaiming blessings abundant for its people. The true church is persecuted by the false church. The true church is made up of people who face life realistically and help people to believe in a loving God *anyway.*

The false doctrine proclaims indirectly that those born in the USA who choose to become Christian have a divine right to a lifetime supply of bread and fish: health, happiness, and freedom from poverty, pain, frustrations, and loneliness. The "crown" gospel teaches that we are a blessed people and a blessed nation. As strange as this may sound, I realized that God is not an American. We are not the chosen few. I was not chosen by God, in my overabundance, to teach others the "crown gospel." I was chosen, as we are all chosen, to persevere in the trials of everyday disappointments and pain. I was chosen, as we all are, to try to understand what it means to be human. Who we really are, what the requirements and possibilities of being human are, and what we should or could be have been questioned and debated, answered and unanswered throughout history. In Jesus, for Christians, an answer — a model, a paradigm of authentic humanity has appeared. The possibilities of human existence are here defined and enacted, and consequently the requirements of being fully human are made plain for the first time.[14] The requirement of being fully human includes pain, sufferings, and finally death. This is the reality of life.

Jesus himself understood what it means to live with serpents and stones. He was scorned by man and forsaken by God. We love the triumphant Christ, but we hate the actual life of the human Christ. Christ's life is too lowly for the self-exalted "crown" gospel that is so prevalent today. It is too lonely and too tragic. This gospel does not prepare us for the harsh, unpleasant realities of life.

I had to face a harsh reality before I was prepared to do so. Why should I have prepared? The "crown" gospel told me that I was exempt. I felt like a school girl walking into a classroom, only to discover that the biggest test of the year had been scheduled for that very day; a student who hadn't so much as opened one book to study and was totally unprepared.

I slowly began to realize that I was not a "chosen" one, but we, who continue on *anyway,* are the chosen many. In my brokenness and humiliation, I started on a long journey of understanding that I am still on, that Christ is the Christ of broken, hurting, humanity. I began to understand that those who must face the harsh, unpleasant realities of life and who are, many times, accused of not having *"enough faith,"*—those who choose to continue to believe in a God of love when their own life is unlovely— are the champions of faith. The walk of the life-worn is the walk of faith. Those who have had to endure already have *"enough faith."* Their faith is greater than that of the people who judge them. The walk of those who demand *"more faith"* from a person who is already hurting is a walk of egotism and religiosity. The person who is hurting is living the faith journey. You who are enduring are already a **HERO** of faith. Those who are broken by the hardships of life are humbled, and in humility lives mirror the life of the historical and biblical Christ:

> *"When pride comes, then comes disgrace,*
> *but with humility comes wisdom."*
> (Proverbs 11:2, NIV)

The pride of those who demand "more faith" from those who are already hurting is disgraceful. Those who have endured being misunderstood and judged have a deep understanding of what faith truly is.

> *"...I served the Lord with great humility*
> *and with tears...."*
> (Acts 20:19,NIV)

Those who have endured hardships understand what it means to serve the Lord with humility and with tears. To serve the Lord with humility and tears includes feeling free to cry out against God sometimes in angry desperation: *"I DON'T UNDERSTAND, GOD! WHERE ARE YOU? DO YOU CARE?"* To serve the Lord with tears is to allow yourself to be real with your feelings. If you're mad at God, tell

Him! If you're tired of being misunderstood, tell Him! If you are too exhausted even to pray anymore, tell Him. The walk of faith includes being able to be honest with your feelings toward God. His shoulder is big enough to handle any emotion you have. Helpless frustration, anger, and disappointment are all human emotions. Any thought that you have you can feel free to express to the One who created wonderful you.

In my realization of total helplessness, I slowly grew from being a queen with a rhinestone crown to a person who could identify with others who are broken, mistreated, misunderstood, and ignored by humanity. Pain has many different names: the Holocaust victim, the cancer patient, the parents who have lost their baby, the child who has suffered physical, sexual, and emotional abuse. The list of different names for pain continues indefinitely, but suffering is still suffering. A person who has experienced one form of pain can identify with another person who has had a different encounter. The inner turmoil, the disappointments, the God-forsakenness are all the same experiences in individual sufferings. Survivors understand each other and speak the same language. One who has had to endure can identify with all of broken, God-forsaken humanity, and once one crosses the bridge of brokenness, all the rhinestones and the faux jewels the world offers lose their seductive power.[15]

I embarked on a faith journey as a reality Christian. For the first time in my life, I could personally understand the intensity of suffering that much of humanity has to endure. My reality included facing an immediate future with the possibility of morbidity and mortality. It meant entering a black hole of suffering, aloneness, anguish, and despair.

"The acceptance of despair is in itself, faith."
Paul Tillich

39

Did I have the faith to say those two words we all hesitate to say, the words that relinquish our will and our future to the will of an unseen God? Could I form the words ...

"Whatever ... God"?

"Whatever happens I will trust you. Whether I live or die, whether I wake up in that cold hospital room able to remember my loved ones names. Whatever happens, whatever path is to be my life's journey, I will trust you."

Yes, I decided I could. Actually not because I was a faith giant, but because at that time in my life I had no other choice! *"Whatever, God,"* are the two most difficult words that human beings can ever utter. In fact, had I not been completely trapped with nowhere else to turn, I could not have said those words at all. I'll admit that at times I said, *"Whatever, God,"* somewhat sarcastically and resentfully. I'll admit that at times I yelled *"Whatever, God,"* in angry desperation. It's not that I thought God wanted to hear those words in order to "prove" to Him that I had "enough faith." In fact, a God who would demand such a declaration during a time of great misery would indeed be a cruel God. I said *"Whatever, God,"* because I was trying to find comfort as I was facing the unknown and the unlovely. Somehow that declaration helped me to feel that God would be with me even though I couldn't feel Him, and it reminded me that in spite of it all, I believe in a God of love.

The new crown I was vying for did not promise a fantasy life of glamour. It wasn't a sparkling, empty dream. It was a crown of painful, terrifying, dark, ugly thorns. It was repulsive to look at. Yet, at closer observation, I realized that though it was cleverly disguised as undesirable, it was full of understanding, compassion, empathy, wisdom, and faith. It's here that the faith journey begins.[16]

Faith is facing reality with courage. Faith is trusting that God is loving in spite of all that seemingly contradicts it. Please understand, this is an incomplete definition of faith. We are just beginning on our journey of understanding. Facing reality with courage doesn't mean that we have to pull ourselves up by our bootstraps and muster all the courage we can to face the wretched times of life; it means first we must allow ourselves to admit that life hurts, that it's scary sometimes, and that praying some magic prayer of faith won't make all of our problems go away. To face reality with courage means to begin looking for practical solutions to problems while choosing to believe that God will help us find practical answers.[17]

Something I found to be very helpful during this time of my life was to choose to believe that someday, if I wanted to, with God's help I could use all of the hurt and frustrations I was experiencing to help someone else survive a trauma in his life. I believe that while in the midst of suffering a valuable tool to use in order to survive is to try to look toward the future and dream of a way that undeserved suffering could possibly be used to help someone else. I am not saying that I believe that people suffer for a purpose, but that a method of survival during a personal holocaust is to imagine a way that hellish times can someday be turned around to help bring a little heaven to another hurting soul.

For example, I know a man named Jim who lives a life of purpose. He was paralyzed in a boating accident ten years ago. The small town where he and his wife Lisa lived didn't have a hospital that could accommodate his needs; so his broken body was flown to another state. At the time of the accident Jim and Lisa were having financial trouble. Because of that, they could not afford to have Lisa stop working in order to be by his side. Consequently, Jim had to face several surgeries and his entire rehabilitation process completely alone. You would think that he would be a bitter man. He certainly has the right to be. Instead, Jim decided that someday he would create something meaningful to help someone else from his own experience of undeserved suffering. He realized

41

that one of the worst parts of his entire ordeal was that he had to go through it all by himself without his lovely wife by his side. He vowed that if he ever met anyone who was facing a similar situation, he would somehow help him financially so that the person suffering would not have to face his pain alone. Although Jim and Lisa still struggle to make ends meet, they try to save fifty cents a day in a jar until they have collected five hundred dollars. Whenever they hear of a person having to face surgery and rehabilitation alone, they mail them the jar money so that a spouse can afford to be by the side of the soul who is hurting during the first week after a trauma. My friends, Jim and Lisa, help to *create* a light in the darkness for others.

I believe that when adversity surrounds us, we have two choices and only two. We either allow the darkness of pain to blacken our entire lives or we dare to dream of a way that a light can be created to shine in the darkness.

"The light shines in the darkness,
and the darkness did not overcome it."
(John 1:5, NRSV)

The mercy of God is found in the fact that goodness can possibly ultimately be created out of the most absurd, undeserved suffering. We can either continue to believe in the love of a good God and choose to create something positive from the negative experiences that all of us will encounter at one time or another, or we can allow self-pity and bitterness to destroy us, which will rob us of the possibility of having a happy and meaningful life in spite of disappointments and frustrations. We can remain in the darkness of pain and frustration or use the pain we've experienced to become a light in the darkness for others.

"They rise in the darkness as a light for the upright;
they are gracious, merciful, and righteous."
(Psa 112:4, NRSV)

42

We can either be angry with the silent God, or we can search to create a purpose for pain and aid God in turning the serpents and stones that randomly come our way into bread and fish to help sustain other people. We can turn hurt into happiness, or we can spend the rest of our lives hurting. We come out of the grindstone of life either chewed up or polished.[18]

BROKEN ILLUSIONS

CHAPTER IV.

**Hope is the only good thing
that disillusion respects.**
Marquis De Vauvenargues

Broken Illusions

The belief that I could eventually create something good from painful experiences gave me the strength I needed to choose to risk my life by having a portion of my brain removed. Pain with purpose is tolerable pain. Please understand that I am not saying that there is some obscure, divine purpose for pain, but that because of the love of God, a glimpse of goodness can be seen at times in the midst of pain, in spite of all that contradicts it, and a good purpose can be created regardless of the absurdities of living in a world of unjust suffering. I made that very difficult decision to go ahead with the surgery, choosing to believe that God would eventually help me create something meaningful for what was purposeless. The ability to create something good out of senseless suffering is possible because of the love of God.

"The Lord said, Surely I will deliver you for a good purpose."
(Jeremiah 15:11, NIV)

I chose to believe that I could use my experiences of pain and suffering to help others become Victors instead of Victims. I am offering this to you as a survival technique that I found helpful while I was facing my own death. Learning to think beyond your current pain toward a day in the future when you can help someone else, will actually give you the hope that tomorrow will be brighter than today. This is the hope of the resurrection in the midst of the crucifixion. It is important to remember that Christ's message of a future beyond death was thoroughly contradicted by the reality of pain and suffering. Yet He had within himself the hope of a tomorrow that enabled Him to face the horror of the day.

As I walked away from my rhinestone crown that was filled with sanguine idealism, I began on a journey toward the cross of pain and suffering that all of humanity will individually bear at one time or another. This journey includes facing the reality of the human predicament, and it will be a journey on which I will continue for the rest of my life. The invitation we have been given by Christ is an invitation to *come and die.* (Heb. 9:27, Col. 2:20, I Cor. 15:31, II Cor. 5: 14,15) The journey toward the cross of reality must include the hope of a brighter day or else we will be crucified by despair alone. Suffering can be a door to the revelation of finding meaning and hope in spite of the painful realities of life.[19]

"At crowning moments of divine revelation,
there has always been suffering;
the cry of the oppressed in Egypt; the cry of Jesus on the cross;
the birth pangs experienced by the whole of creation
as it awaits liberation."[20]

The rhinestone crown of idealism represents the belief that those who trust in God will have a soft and protected life full of "blessings from God." This crown symbolizes traditional westernized Christianity.[21] Its doctrine indirectly teaches that we must attain a certain amount of visible success, raise perfect children, and have a happily-ever-after marriage just to enter the doors of a church to worship, only to find the service full of dignified clergy, entertainers, and a perfectly planned service making a person feel that somehow, he or she doesn't measure up.

This is a distorted gospel. I know this doctrine very well. It is the doctrine I represented in my beauty pageant days of wearing a crown on my head and quoting Proverbs 3:4-5. I realize now that I wasn't giving anyone the tools needed to survive in an unfair world by merely proclaiming a theology of rhinestones. Instead, I was representing an unrealistic approach to life. It was unintentional. At the time I thought that I was presenting the biblical gospel that would help others and this is a trap that many people and churches fall into. It seems innocent enough, but it's important to remember that Jesus never claimed to be a king of glamorous earthly glory, but the King of broken humanity. Jesus didn't escape the reality of our human situation, but embraced it and then offered us hope beyond the dark night of suffering. I do believe in a quality presentation of the gospel, but I advocate that it is important to be sure we are consistently presenting the correct message, the message of the Crucified Christ of hope, not the idealistic crown gospel that I had been guilty of portraying.

The crown gospel is twisted, cold, and dead when presented as truth. It is a fraudulent declaration of rhinestones (an imitation of value, yet holding no value of its own) and false pretenses. It's attractive, but it's worthless.

"Religion has long been criticized for fostering man's desire to avoid the hard truths in favor of the soft lie."
Unknown

When I speak of the journey to the cross, I mean facing one's own personal mortality. This is the journey we are all on though we seldom realize it. Life will culminate in death. Death is what we live for, yet somehow we think *"I will never be the one who will die."*

The journey to the cross entails embarking on a road of reality, knowing that life will, in fact, end, yet, continuing to embrace the promise of a new day. To *"come and die"* means to walk away from delusions and to face the realities of life while remembering that the resurrection is our hope for tomorrow. We can continue to possess the power of hope while we endure with dignity and humility the crosses (the problems) we have, because we've chosen to search for a way that a purpose can be created from the purposeless.[22]

49

"Therefore I run in such a way, as not without aim."
(I Cor. 9:26, NAS)

We run toward hope. It is through this journey that we can choose to learn compassion and empathy as we begin to identify with all of broken humanity.

"...If any one wishes to come after Me, let him deny himself, and take up his cross, and follow Me."
(Matt. 16:24, NAS)

My illusions were broken; the preliminary pageant of pain began. I knew the journey would be painful and terrifying. I knew there would be tremendous suffering. Yet it was my only hope for survival. I knew I was dying. I believe the thing that tortured me the most was that I was absolutely powerless to do anything in the midst of suffering, but to endure more suffering. I felt alone and abandoned. I even felt angry with God that He was seemingly sitting on the sidelines in apathy while I was desperately hurting. The suffering of Jesus became increasingly intriguing. Was it possible for God to identify with my fear and aloneness?

The organized church tends to stress the divinity of Christ so much that His identification with humanity gets lost in the shuffle of religion. The concept of God being completely human is extremely difficult for us to grasp, yet this dualism is the wonder of the entire Christian doctrine.[23] It is the ultimate paradox. Webster defines paradox as: *"a statement that seems contrary to common sense, yet is perhaps true."* How can the God of all creation, the God who is all knowing, all seeing, all powerful, limit himself to a creature He created;[24] a creature that cannot grasp the truths of the universe;[25] a creature that feels frightened, alone, forsaken, forgotten, and even punished by God? How is it possible for the divine Son of God and a man who must doubt the very existence of God in order to completely identify with us, to live in the same body?[26] How incredible. How unbelievable. How perfect! This concept — God in human form, complete human form — must include doubting His own divinity.[27] Otherwise, He could not possibly totally identify with our broken humanity.

"His state was divine, yet he did not cling to his equality with God but emptied Himself to assume the condition of a slave, and became as men are, he was humbler yet, even to accepting death, death on a cross." [28]

(Phil 2: 5-8)

Theologian Christian Kettler, one of my favorite professors in graduate school, calls this inconceivable notion, "the vicarious humanity of Christ."[29] Vicarious, according to Webster means: *"To experience sympathetically."* In order for God to sympathetically experience the human predicament, the despair, the aloneness, the suffering, the fear, the doubt, He would have to become human, thus allowing himself to doubt His own divine existence.[30] With this concept, Jesus, the man, became my confidante, my friend. My personal faith began to intertwine with the faith of the man of Nazareth. I began to study His most agonizing moments. Did He really know despair and isolation? The accounts of the Garden of Gethsemane and on the cross at Calvary say "yes" He did. Let us assume this is true. If it is, then there is much to learn from the life of this man. The most important is the insight that we gain from that which crowns the life of Jesus.

What did He spend His life preparing to do? He lived to wear a crown of thorns, to suffer and to die in order to identify with and redeem humanity. Because of the example of the life of Jesus one can choose to suffer purposefully even though the pain itself is undeserved.[31] If suffering was the culmination of the human life of the Son of God, then shouldn't we, as those who follow Him, take a serious look at the possibility of creating a positive purpose from sufferings rather than spend our lives denying their reality?

51

By denying them, I mean we never really believe suffering will happen to us — until it does. Then, we are left sorely equipped to handle the realities of life. *I know I was.*

To begin the journey I studied the Christ theme: When the universe is drowning with the senselessness of suffering, when the whole world cries for explanation that no man of flesh can give, what is one to do?[32] Christ is our reassurance that suffering unjustly is God-like. He is our hope that God is in the midst of the God-forsaken and abandoned. To see the face of Jesus on the Cross helps us to be able to forgive God for the presence of injustice and evil in this world. Do I really mean forgive God? Isn't that blasphemy to even suggest such an idea? No! I believe that in Jesus, God had to bear the painful grief of indirectly causing suffering. How is this possible? God causing suffering? Yes, it certainly seems contradictory to say that a creator is not responsible, in some sense, for the origin of evil.[33] To acquit God or apologize for Him when unjust suffering is so prevalent would be demeaning God's power and denying His omnipotence. A theodicy of protest is not only human, but also healthy. *(Theodicy is the term theologians use when addressing the problematic belief of an all-powerful God who continues to allow existence of evil.)* It's all right to blame God and be angry with God when bad things happen to good people. Your cry against God is a cry for justice. Humankind cannot be fully blamed for the presence of evil in the world; it was not man who initiated history. God must bear His share of responsibility, and He grieves in His own acceptance of that responsibility. He suffers in the knowledge that He created us and we suffer.

> *"And the Lord was sorry that He had made man on the earth, and He was grieved in His heart."*
>
> (Genesis 6:6, NKJ)

52

If He had not created us, we would not be suffering. This is what I suggest by saying that God *indirectly* causes our suffering.[34] I want to make it clear that I am not exclusively referring to dramatic physical ailments when I address the issue of suffering. Rather, I am addressing the issue of pain and suffering in general; the pain of loneliness, the pain of the experience of Nothing answering when we pray, the pain of disappointment, the pain of frustration, the pain of being unfairly treated, and the pain of simply being human and having to live in an imperfect world where God seems to be silent.

I believe that praise and protest walk hand in hand, for the other side of protest is belief. In accusing God we declare His presence, for why bother trying to defend something or someone that doesn't exist? In other words, it's okay to be angry with God sometimes. It's all right to yell in rebellion against undeserved suffering. If God is large enough to create a world, die for our sins, redeem humanity, and still be ultimately responsible for the existence of evil, then He is large enough to sustain the blows of our tiny fists as we beat against His mighty chest in questioning rebellion. Anger toward God in itself is not wrong. It's only when we hold onto anger day after day, month after month, year after year, without trying to search for a loving God beyond the hurt, that our anger becomes sin. It is then that anger can turn into bitterness, which is detrimental to us and to those around us.

> *"Be angry but do not sin; do not let the sun go*
> *down on your anger."*
> (Eph 4:26, NRSV)

Is there comfort to be found beyond the anger? Can we ever dare to hope that a loving God exists after experiencing a personal holocaust? Dietrich Bonhoeffer, the famous German theologian who died at the hands of Nazi soldiers in a concentration camp, believed that only the suffering God can possibly help.[35] In other words, only a God who can identify with pain because He has

53

personally experienced it can be trusted. This is why I believe that our understanding of who God is must begin with the concept of the Crucified God. The cross screams for us our cry against a good God who allows suffering and evil. The cross is the full, undisguised, bitterness towards God and the reality of the abandonment of God. The desertion on Good Friday is where faith begins. I can truthfully and soberly say that I know God because I have been abandoned by God. Because of the relevance of the Christ of the Cross I can honestly accuse God and stand before Him in humble awe at the same time.

One of the most helpful responses to suffering came from the pen of Bonhoeffer while he was in a Nazi prison:

> *"Time is never wasted when one is suffering.*
> *Suffering is the highest school of learning."*

Catch this. This is very important. Bonhoeffer is not saying that suffering is the boot camp of God to whip people into shape for some abstract eternal plan; rather, he is suggesting that if we choose to search for something beyond our current experience, we are somehow linked back to a higher ground of meaning.[36] The cross is and continues to be the unequivocal revelation of the world's estrangement.[37] Suffering is the bridge between the earthly and the heavenly, the temporary and the eternal. The cross on Calvary is the marriage between the human and the divine. It is the symbol of human existence with all of its collective suffering having meaning in the eternal plan with all of its glory.

Please understand, this theology is very different, in fact opposite, from the mistaken theology that God strikes people, as if with a lightening bolt, to punish or force individuals to go through personal hardships for some abstract eternal plan.[38] Rather, I am stating that we live in an imperfect world in which bad things happen to good people through no fault of their own, and that individual suffering results simply because of the fact that we live in a flawed world.[39] When I address the suffering of humankind, I am referring to the pain that humanity endures collectively. Though suffering is universal, we have a choice of how we react to adversity individually. We can choose to be pitifully bitter, or we can use the pain that randomly comes our way as a springboard toward creating a positive purpose. In other words, hell can be used as a launching pad toward heaven.

Why is there unjust suffering in a world that a loving God created? That agonizing question is as old as time itself. *Qualis sit deus?* "What kind of God is this?" is the cry suffering humanity has yelled up to the heavens throughout the centuries. How can a Creator who claims to love His creation enough to personally suffer and die for its redemption continue to allow His children to live in a world of unwarranted suffering and excruciating pain? The traditional theology of sanguine hope that the organized church clings to all too often dwells on the resurrection of Christ at the expense of ignoring the implications of the crucifixion. This is the core of the misguided theology that is within the evangelical community. Merely proclaiming the resurrection of Christ, the victory, and the defeat of the grave, belittles the importance of what took place at Golgotha. If, however, our theology begins at the cross, then hope that surpasses suffering is revealed.[40] This hope contains the peace of God that surpasses all comprehension. (Phil. 4:7)

In other words, to live with true hope is to always take the painful realities of life seriously. A theology such as the "health and wealth" gospel that tries to avoid the stark, agonizing realities of living in a world where suffering is abundant, is empty. Transcendent hope (hope beyond current sufferings) is actually found at the cross because it transcends, not avoids, not exempts, not explains, but rather transcends human agony.[41] The theology of the cross that accepts the realities of pain and suffering prepares us for the battles of life in an imperfect world.[42]

55

Throughout the ages many different philosophers and theologians have theorized as to whether there is a purpose behind suffering. As we remember the book of Job in the Bible we will recall Job's friends trying desperately to find a reason for the fact that Job was suffering. Surely Job had done something to deserve it, one friend offered. (Job 8) Maybe he was morally defective, another suggested. (Job 11) Maybe he was downright wicked, implied another. (Job 15 and 18) Possibly, he was cruel to the poor. (Job 20) Maybe God was disciplining Job, cried another. (Job 36) As the story continues we discover that while God does not offer an explanation as to exactly why Job suffered, God did reveal that he was not pleased with the pious explanations of Job's friends:

> *"My wrath is kindled against you and against your*
> *two friends, because you have not spoken of me*
> *what is right as my servant Job has."*
>
> (Job 42: 7, NAS)

Job's friends are still alive and well today. People who try to find a "divine" reason for *why* someone is suffering unjustly are Job's friends. If you have had anyone try to tell you that you are suffering because you must have done something wrong, or because there is sin in your life, or because God is trying to make you stronger, or because you are in need of *"more faith,"* then try to remember, as hurtful as those judgments can be, that God was angry with Job's friends and their poor counsel. If you are suffering right now or have had to endure pain and suffering in the past, then you are a hero of faith. **Hold your head high!**

All of humanity will eventually face pain and disappointments of one type or another. The message in the Bible is clear on this subject.

> *"Since Christ has suffered in the flesh,*
> *arm yourselves also with the same purpose."*
>
> (1 Peter 4:1, NAS)

The fact is, it hurts to be human. The purpose of the church is to bear one another's burdens, not to judge people who are hurting or to demand *"more faith."* We must simply build up each other in love and recognize that those who are suffering and still choosing to believe in a loving God are living a life of faith.

"Though He slay me, yet will I trust Him."
(Job 13:15, NKJ)

Imprisoned in Pain

Throughout all of the rebuilding process of my theology, I would pray day after day in desperate physical pain and Nothing would still answer. It was time to assume the responsibility of possibly finding a solution to my life-altering dilemma. I began to compare neurosurgeons around the country who performed this operation. I soon discovered that this particular surgery was so new that it is only performed in a small number of hospitals around the world. I began to collect information about the various surgeons, trying to find the ones who had performed the most surgeries of this particular kind each year and how their success records compared to one another.

National statistics stated a significant percentage of morbidity and mortality. The percentage was significant enough that I chose to write a living will in order to save my family as much grief as possible should I die or become an invalid. I discovered three hospitals that claimed the highest success rate for this particular type of brain surgery, specifically for this illness called epilepsy, and chose one of the three randomly. The morning of December 2, I called the hospital, sent my medical records, and waited for a return call to see if they could help. Four days later I had a surgery date for January 21 and I began to feel a certain amount of excitement. I thought, *"After January 21 I will be healed! The horror will finally be over!"* In a way, I was looking forward to the surgery, thinking that it meant an end to three painful years.

Three weeks of hope passed. Then, on a cold Tuesday morning in early January, the phone rang. A representative from Epilepsy Kansas, who knew that I had decided on the surgery, was on the other end of the line.

"Hi, Teri!" she said. "I heard you have scheduled the *first* surgery for this month. You will know immediately following the first surgery if you are a candidate for the *big one!*"

Wait a minute ... *the first surgery?... You mean that I have to have two brain surgeries?*

I thought that surely this had to be a mistake. Surely this person did not know what she was talking about. Surely she had me confused with someone else. I quickly called the hospital to confirm.

"Yes, of course, Ms. Messner. The first surgery is to help us determine if we can even perform the second surgery which could possibly help you."

"How dangerous is the first surgery?" I asked, not wanting to hear the reply.

"There are significant risks," the cold voice answered.

I numbly hung up the phone, paralyzed in disbelief. As the reality began to sink in, all the pain that I had lived with for the last three years suddenly flooded my heart, soul, and future in one horrendous moment. Racking sobs began to overtake me in the realization of my complete helplessness.

I had embarked on the journey of a reality Christian, but this was too much reality, too soon! The grief gradually melted into anger, and I began to ask the question that plagues all of humanity at one time or another:

"Why Me?"

What had I done to deserve all of this torment, disappointment, and anguish? I had thought that I could handle one brain surgery, that I could face paralysis and death once, but not twice! I felt singled out, almost as if my life had been predestined for pain and disappointment. Everyone around me seemed to have such a happy, "normal" existence, that I felt alone, forsaken, forgotten, and yes, even punished by God. Were there any answers?

"WHY ME, GOD?"

WHY ME? ... WHY YOU?

CHAPTER V

*I am not afraid of storms for I am
learning how to sail my ship.*
Louisa May Alcott

Why Me?...Why You?

Why Me?

*P*rimary insight was revealed to me on the twenty-first of January when I was admitted into the hospital. Not only was I to share a wing with other individuals who were scheduled to have the same exploratory surgery, but I was also just one of hundreds of patients in that particular hospital, at that particular time. All were there for a wide variety of illness ranging from diabetes to cancer to heart disease. The list of illnesses goes on and on. As I looked around me at all the suffering that was so abundant, my question of *"why me?"* transposed into: *"Why not me?"*

Why not me? For some reason, I had thought that suffering would only happen to *other* people. Only *other* people become sick, only *other* people actually die. Why?... Why did I assume I would be exempt from pain? Jesus suffered severely. Why did I think that I shouldn't or wouldn't? Why not me?

Suffering is a part of living in this absurd and wonderful world. Yes, I believe that a loving God created this world. Yes, God is sovereign, so the good and the bad are all under God's authoritative hand, but why? Why does a loving God allow so much suffering? If God is sovereign, which tradition and scripture informs us that He is, then all good and evil are in His ultimate control and no one is exempt.

> *"(God) sends rain on the*
> *righteous and the unrighteous."*
> (Matt. 5:45, NIV)

But why? Are there reasons? Why you? Why have you had bad things happen to you? Is there a reason? More importantly, is there purpose for what you have had to endure?

Why You?

How many times have you asked God that agonizing question? Why have you had to suffer disappointments, physical pain, mental anguish, and emotional hurt? Why has your life been so hard? Why couldn't it all have happened to someone else? Why you? You're a good person. Yes, you are! You've tried hard to live a good life. What did you ever do to deserve such hard times in life? Why you?

Some people would think that asking *"why?"* is, in itself, a contradiction of faith. Were we not taught in the traditional church that to believe in a personal God who is always working in our lives for our ultimate good means to not question Him?[43]

If we believe that God is a God of love, then does asking *"why?"* demonstrate a lack of faith? Doesn't it? Does it? I say emphatically, NO! I believe that when we cry out *"why me?"* we are asking for justification from a God that we want to believe is a just God. We are crying out for God to answer why there is so much undeserved suffering in this world. We are unconsciously admitting to ourselves that, in spite of it all, we believe that God is a God of purpose and that God is a God of love.

"Why me, God?" is actually the verbalization of asking for an explanation of why there is so much unjust suffering. *"Why, why, why?"* we all cry out to an unseen God. The cry of why is really the cry of faith. Why even ask *"why?"* if we believe that God is a cruel, uncaring, purposeless Creator? When we ask this question, we are unconsciously admitting that we believe in a God who cares enough to love us as individuals. Indeed, asking *"why?"* is actually the beginning of our putting faith into action.

So is God a just God? Does God care about you? Are you special to Him?

Yes.

> *"Before I formed you in the womb, I knew you.*
> *Before you were born, I set you apart."*
> (Jeremiah 1:5, NIV)

Were you "struck down" for some future good purpose?

> *"...all things work together for good for those who love God,*
> *who are called according to His purpose."*
> (Romans 8:28, NRS)

No! This scripture does not mean that you or I were specifically struck, as if by a lightning bolt, by God to suffer for some vague mysterious purpose out of the blue somewhere. A loving God wouldn't use lightning bolts to make people suffer in order to create a good purpose someday. Not at all! It means that God can work all things out eventually for good in spite of the absurd evil in this imperfect world. When we cry out to God for explanation we are beginning to confess that deep down in the innermost part of our souls, we believe in a God who is good.

Once I established this in my own mind, I began a search to find the answer to two primary questions:

- Why was I suffering so severely?
- Why is there so much suffering in a world that a loving God created?

I began by asking all the "right" people, who gave me empty answers. I sought advice from family members, friends, pastors, and theologians. I discovered that when a person begins to seek advice from other people, she opens herself up to a bombardment of "pat" answers and sometimes severe judgment. Job's friends are definitely still around trying to "help." One individual told me:

65

"You should be grateful for what you have. There are so many people hurting much more than you are. Count your blessings. If you will just begin to look around, you'll start counting your lucky stars that you don't have the problems that other people have."

What this person didn't realize is he was taking away my "right" to hurt. In addition to all the disappointments and the physical anguish, I was supposed to feel guilty because I wasn't suffering as much as someone else? It was this "pat" answer that helped me to realize that we can't compare pain. We all have something in common. Every one of us, at one time or another will experience some form of pain. Pain comes in many different forms:

- Emotional
- Physical
- Mental
- Spiritual

Your pain is different from my pain. Pain has many different names. Maybe yours is a physical problem. Possibly you have a closet full of terrible memories that you are trying to put to rest. Maybe you were abused at some time in your life. Have you lost someone you loved deeply? Is someone else you love hurting? You are still hurting for them, aren't you? Maybe you are insecure and feel as though your life doesn't matter. We can't compare pain. Although our pain is different, the fact that we have all experienced disappointment with life and feelings that life just isn't fair helps us to identify with each other. Everyone can identify with pain, so we can begin to understand each other, but we can't compare our individual sufferings. When it's your pain it hurts you and it's painful. Right? **You have a right to your pain!**

When someone says, *"Count your blessings. Compared to other people, you're lucky,"* they take away your right to be disappointed when bad things happen to you. All of us have our own load to carry. We all have individual burdens.

> *"For each one should carry his own load."*
> (Gal. 6:5, NIV)

When it is your burden, it's heavy, isn't it? It hurts, doesn't it? Your pain is important. Yes, it is!

Once I had acknowledged that it was okay for me to feel disappointed, to feel that I had somehow been cheated in life, I resigned myself to the fact that for now, anyway, my daily existence was filled with pain. I knew that I could not deny the realities of life any longer. I was simply not going to get better. It was time to be brave enough to face reality. My reality included having a part of my brain removed. Many people assume that this surgery is to remove a growth or a tumor. This is not the case. There wasn't a growth of any kind, just simply overactive brain cells that were destroying my life.

The first surgery took place on the twenty-first of January. Two dime-size holes were drilled through my skull on either side of my face, where my cheeks meet my ears. Electrodes (wires that are to interpret impulses from the brain) were placed underneath my skull, on top of my brain. They were left there for three, twenty-four hour days and I was monitored. We waited for seizures. My brain cooperated, and I had four seizures within the three-day period. The neurosurgeon told me that he had all the information he needed and that the seizures were definitely coming from the tip of the right temporal lobe and could be eliminated with surgery. The electrodes were removed and the second surgery was scheduled for six weeks later. I was sent home to recover. I had survived the first surgery!

I remember remarking to my husband on the long trip home from the hospital, *"Well, I have survived one brain surgery. What's one more?"*

I am still thankful that we are not able to see into the future. I'm thankful that I had no idea, at that time, what was ahead of me and was about to happen to me.

During those six weeks in between, I returned to my thirsty search to find the answer to the question, *"Why me?"* I was still holding onto the "crown gospel" that is deeply ingrained in all of us.

Someone thought he had the answer. This letter arrived, unsigned. It read:

Dear Teri,

If you would get your life straight with the Lord, He would stop punishing you. Satan is really in your life. You need to pray for forgiveness. If you only had enough faith, God would heal you! You are showing your lack of faith by continuing to take medicine and by planning to have surgery. God won't help you until you have faith. You just aren't accepting your healing. I pray for you to have faith enough to accept your healing.

In Christ's love,
A friend

I'll admit, as I first read the contents of this note I felt angry at the injustice of being blamed for having to endure living with a physical ailment and then being judged for not having *"enough faith."* The anger gradually melted into feelings of hurt and frustration. How could someone be so insensitive and cruel and be doing it in the name of God? I gradually began to learn that being misunderstood is just part of the journey.

Shortly after I had received this note, two friends told me about their encounter with this misguided theology. This gospel has been referred to as the "name it and claim it" or the "health and wealth" gospel. It proclaims that a person can have health and prosperity if he or she attains *enough faith*. It teaches that God wants to give us

68

our hearts' desires, but we must learn how to have faith *enough* to accept them.

Because of my friends' experience and my own, I now refer to this warped gospel that is preached to people who must live with physical maladies as the gospel of ***blaming the victims.*** My friends' stories are important because similar scenarios are taking place every day all over the country. The following chapter is an account of the events as they were told to me. I will be using the conservative charismatic language that's prevalent when healing issues are addressed in religious settings.

BLAMING THE VICTIMS

CHAPTER VI

We have just enough religion to make us hate, but not enough to make us love one another.
Jonathan Swift

Blaming the Victims

*B*ob Shervly pounded the podium as if to drive the words he was saying into the very souls of each person present.

"I have good news for you this morning. God's will is that all humans are in perfect health - mentally, spiritually, and physically. Illness is not a part of God's plan. Whoever is physically afflicted is so because they do not have enough faith or have not accepted their healing from God. People who become ill are not living the true Christian life. The true Christian life is a life of blessing. Psalms 103:3 says:

> *'Bless the Lord ... who pardons all your iniquities;*
> *Who heals all your diseases.'"* (NAS)

Three rows back sat Alan Weber. Alan had recently been diagnosed with cancer. With each word Bob spoke, Alan's heart began to beat faster. His nails almost pierced the flesh of his hand as he was trying to control the rage of injustice in his heart. His other hand tightly clenched his Bible.

A memory of a warm summer night flashed through his mind when he had attended a healing service. He felt confident that this was what God was calling him to do, for three months earlier he had been diagnosed as having cancer of the colon which had already spread to the surrounding nodes. He remembered walking to the altar with tears streaming down his face to humbly kneel and to be anointed with healing oil. For a former professional football player, the moment had been quite humbling, yet, somehow fulfilling at the same time. Bob had knelt with him to pray that night. After the service Alan remembered walking outside to witness a sky filled with beautiful shining stars. It had been raining before the service began. Alan interpreted this as a confirmation of healing from God. His heart was full of thankfulness and joy. He proclaimed to all who would hear that he had been divinely healed.

The phone ran sharply at 8:00 a.m. the next morning. Dr. Caroline Bradshaw had bad news to tell him.

"We have just received the report from your last tests. The cancer has spread. You will need to schedule an appointment to begin chemotherapy treatment."

Alan's reply was confident:

"I appreciate your concern, but God has healed me."

Dr. Bradshaw gently replied:

"Alan, I am a Christian too. I believe God uses modern medicine to heal people. The Bible says, *'All wisdom is of God.'* What is medical science but advanced wisdom? I believe medical science is wisdom to heal that God has allowed us to have. It is a tool God uses to perform His miracles. I believe that all healing, including human assisted healing, is divine. Please come in and let us do one more scan."

Alan answered, "I'll come just to prove to you that I have been healed!"

That afternoon Alan lay on the examination table with great excitement. He could hardly wait to hear the words, "We can't find a trace of cancer! You are healed!"

The minutes passed, ever so slowly. Finally, Dr. Bradshaw walked into the room. Her face was heavy with a knowledge she did not want to share. Gently, she reached over to touch Alan's arm.

"I'm sorry, Alan. The cancer has spread further. Please remember what I said about medical science being God's tool. We can start treatment tomorrow."

Disappointment and sorrow filled Alan's soul.

"Why, God? I had faith," he prayed silently.

Then a glimmer of hope returned to his heart. He continued his silent prayer:

"You promised me that I was healed, yet you didn't promise how you would heal me. I know you are faithful to me, so I will be faithful to you. This is not the form of healing I wanted, but I will accept your answer of healing through medical science."

After arriving home, he immediately called the prayer chain and explained the circumstances. They faithfully fasted and prayed along with him for his complete healing.

Three days later a note arrived in the mail from a dear friend of his. The scripture enclosed was Jeremiah 29:11.

"For I know the plans I have for you, says the Lord. They are plans for good and not for evil, to give you a future and a hope."
(The Living Bible)

Once again, he felt God was confirming his healing. Four hopeful weeks passed. It was time again for another scan. His dreams were dashed when Dr. Bradshaw announced that, once again, the cancer had spread. The treatments had been ineffective.

Alan fell to his knees and wept tears of frustration and disappointment. He prayed, *"Father, don't let me die. By the blood of Jesus, in the name of Jesus, please heal my wounds."*

Alan knew the Bible well. The last few weeks he had especially been studying the sufferings of Jesus. He began recalling what Jesus had said as He was praying in the Garden of Gethsemane in great agony as He was facing the cross. Alan remembered that Jesus had begged God to *"take this cup from me."* (Mark 14:36, NIV) Then Bob recalled the words Jesus had said after His plea for divine intervention:

"Yet not what I will, but what you will." (Mark 14:36, NIV) After a moment Alan lowered his head and prayed his prayer of faith:

"Father, thank you for sending your Son. I will follow His example. I still have faith. Let your will be done so that you will be glorified in my life or in my death. If you want me to live, I will live faithfully. If it is your will that I am healed by dying, then I will die faithfully. I will endure faithfully. For you are God, no matter what happens."

"By His wounds you are healed!"

Bob's resounding voice brought Alan back to the reality of the Sunday school class.

"You must claim in faith that you are healed!" Bob continued.

Sitting beside Alan was Jan Cambel. Jan was sitting in a wheelchair, a victim of polio from childhood. Alan reached out to grab Jan's hand as if to say, *"I understand your frustration. We will endure this injustice together."* She had been prayed for, anointed with oil, and had "claimed in faith" her healing on countless occasions. She vividly remembered a particular time during such a service that she had been so positive she was healed, that she had asked two people to help her stand to claim her healing. The result had been devastating when her legs immediately crumbled under her. Yet, in spite of unanswered prayers, she knew in her heart that God loved her. She trusted her future to Him completely. Now this man, who had never experienced any form of physical affliction other than the flu, was condemning her for not having enough faith! Uncontrollable tears streamed down her face.

Alan stood up, placed one hand on Jan's shoulder and gently said, "I can't agree with you, Bob. The Bible does not promise faith-filled Christians will escape all suffering. Do you recall the

76

scripture, *'It rains on the righteous and the unrighteous'*? (Matt. 5:45) In fact, the Bible gives account after account of saints suffering and enduring. God promises to give strength to the weary and will reward those who suffer unjustly."

Bob's reply was, "Deut. 7:15 states, *'You will be blessed more than any other people. The Lord will keep you free from every disease.'* Are you denying God's word, Alan?"

Alan could bear no more. He bowed his head, shook his shoulders in silent resignation and whispered tearfully in Jan's ear. "Remember the word's of Jesus: *'Father, forgive them, for they do not know what they are doing.'*" (Luke 23:34, NIV)

With that, he took a deep breath, straightened his shoulders and wheeled Jan out of the room. Being misunderstood is, indeed, part of the faith journey.

Alan and Jan came to me seeking reassurance. They felt humiliated to have basically been labeled "faithless" in a room full of healthy people. They were frustrated, hurt, and angry. Both had faithfully believed that they would be healed by the "blood of Christ." Bob had blamed Alan for the cancer that continued to rage on, and he had blamed Jan for her disability. I asked myself, *"Does Jesus blame the victims of disease in this unjust world? What does the Bible have to say?"* Sadly this scenario is being repeated countless times in churches all over the world.

I was also a victim of this theology of denial of suffering and our vulnerability as human beings. Epilepsy is a misunderstood illness. I would have never believed, had I not experienced it myself, that some people, even church clergy, believe that epilepsy is a sign of demonic possession. It still amazes me that this ignorance is so prevalent. A friend of mine who grew up in West Virginia and went to a private "Christian" school has had epilepsy since birth. During her school age years she was teased unmercifully by other students and treated as though she were demon-possessed by a particular teacher. Every time that teacher would pass her in the hallway, he would point his finger at her and yell, *"In the name of Jesus, I command the satanic demon in Connie's body that causes her to seizure to leave her at once and go where the Lord Jesus Christ sends it."* Can you imagine what that would do to a child's self-image?

Once a minister screamed in my face, *"I cast you, Satan, out of Teri in the name of Jesus, by the blood of Jesus."* I was told by a clergy member of a church that "yes, the Bible does seem to indicate that epilepsy is a symptom of demonic possession."

The passage in the Bible that has led people to believe this atrocity is found in Matthew 17:14-20. Here the disciple recounts an event of a man bringing a boy to Jesus to be healed of an "unclean spirit" that forced the boy to:

"convulse ... scream ... become mute ... foam at the mouth ... grit his teeth ... fall into the water and the fire ... and become dead, like a corpse."

The original Greek passages say **nothing** of the boy having the illness called epilepsy. They simply refer to the boy having convulsions of some type. How these passages were translated into epilepsy can only be explained as misinterpretation and misunderstanding. The original Greek[44] passage actually translates, word for word, as follows:

Kurio's, Koo'ree-os: from Kuros (supremacy) supreme in authority. implies Mr. (as a respectful title) God , Lord, Master, Sir.
Eleeo, el,eh, eh'-o: compassionate (by word, by divine grace, have compassion (pity on) have mercy.
Huios: a son remote or figurative kinship, child, son.
Seleniazomai: to be moonstruck. i.e. crazy: be lunatic.
Kakos, Kakoce: badly amiss, diseased, grievously, miserably sick, sore.
Pascho-pas'kho: to experience a sensation, impression (usually painful) feel passion, suffer.
Pollakis: many times, frequently.
Pipto: to fall down.
pur: fiery

In one sentence, the Greek could actually translate: *"Lord, have compassion and mercy. My son has been struck by the moon and is miserably sick and sore. He experiences painful sensations and suffers frequently and falls down."* (Implying a convulsion)

In reality, many illnesses can cause one to experience convulsions. These include diabetic reactions, low blood sugar, electrolyte imbalances, hypoxia, tumors, and cardiac arthythmias among multiple others. It is also extremely common for children under the age of three to experience benign febrile seizures.

At this particular time in history, the Christian expositors blamed all disease on evil spirits and the moon. While their judgments have been invalidated by modern medicine, one must recognize that their motive was the preservation of God's goodness. By assigning an illness to demons, they were setting God against sickness.

Christian teaching maintains that Jesus was fully human and fully divine. This is called the hypostatic union — the union of two natures in one person. It makes sense to believe that the human Jesus was limited to the knowledge and the culture of His day. On the other hand, if we were to choose to believe that Jesus did possess infinite knowledge, we must remember that all illness during the time He walked the earth was considered evil humor. While in the process of healing the sick, He could not have stopped to explain the medical reasons for physical illness. Just imagine what the reaction would have been in the Roman Empire days if He had paused and explained the medical details behind the illness of each victim He met. Instead, Christ did the most practical thing he could do by simply using the language and cultural understanding of that period in history. Remember Jesus walked the earth long before blood tests, CT scans, heart monitors, EEGs, sonograms, or antibiotics were invented! It's tragic, with the twenty-first Century knowledge of the disease process, that some people still hold on to the antediluvian definitions of illness.

It is historical ignorance that labeled physical illness as a sign of demon possession and uninformed translators that labeled the child's convulsion as being pure epilepsy. As stated, the convulsions could have been caused from a number of diseases. Ill-informed translators gave the child the diagnosis of epilepsy without medical understanding of the multitude of other causes of convulsions. It saddens me to have witnessed and endured the judgment of being "demon possessed" by overemotional and ill-informed Christians. I am especially disappointed when I encounter this in clergy members who have been supposedly trained to try to correctly interpret scripture. It is illogical that some uninformed Christians label those who must endure the physical disability of epilepsy as being demon possessed, yet believe that a convulsion due to an insulin reaction is "just medicine."

This type of judgment is not, as we have seen, exclusively pronounced on people who have seizures. The "blaming the victim" mind-set has victimized people all over the world for all different forms of physical illness. This malignant mentality is spreading rapidly and is a direct result of the distorted and crippling "name it and claim it, health-wealth, prosperity gospel" that is filtering into churches all over the world. There are many powerful religious leaders who are preaching this treacherous doctrine, and the virus is continuing to spread rapidly.

These so-called "faith teachers" are not only viciously blaming the victims of disease, but they even have the audacity to blame people who are poor for not having faith enough to accept the blessings that God wants to give them. They claim that poverty is a sin and a spirit that can be broken with a pledge of faith. Of course, the way to "prove" this faith so that one can be healthy and wealthy is to send a "pledge of faith" to the faith teachers themselves. ($1,000.00 seems to be the magic number.)[45] The faith teachers have a great scam going.

The problem with this counterfeit theology is that the people who proclaim it are taking scriptures out of context and are using them as a weapon to defend their own personal beliefs. As far as the faith teachers are concerned, they are preaching it to make themselves rich!

Hank Hanegraaff, in his book *Christianity In Crisis,* addresses this extremely important issue by quoting the dangerous heretical sludge of the so-called Faith Teachers who are proclaiming these errant teachings. I urge anyone who has been a victim of this religious cancer and who is wrestling with this issue to listen to the audio version of this timely book. You'll be amazed at what you will hear from the lips of the faith teachers themselves and how cruel this counterfeit theology is. Hanegraaff explains this deadly doctrine:

> *The faith teachers teach people to have faith in faith rather than faith in God...The faith teachers teach that faith is a force and words are the containers of the force thus through the power of words you can create your own reality...The faith teachers induct themselves into the faith hall of fame and then take someone like a Job and induct him into a faith hall of shame. When God calls Job upright the faith teachers call him carnal. When God calls Job good, the faith teachers call him bad. When God says "Job has spoken right" the faith teachers say that Job made a negative confession... The truth is that Job is right and the faith teachers are wrong... In Job 1:22 God says "in all of this Job did not sin." ...The faith teachers have taken the fabric of faith and torn it to shreds.*[46]

Illness is a problem because of Christian cowardice. People who resort to blaming the victims of disease are actually themselves trying to find a reason for illness so that they will feel protected and exempt. The problem of suffering should be redefined as a problem that some people have in accepting suffering and death as the harsh realities of life. It is difficult to accept how fragile we are because then *"we"* become as vulnerable as *"they."* This denial of suffering and blaming victims derives from an exclusive mind-set that is very similar to the "crown" gospel. Those who adopt this mentality try to delude themselves into believing that they are personally excluded from illness and death because of their righteousness. People who proclaim this flawed faith theology use such phrases as *"healing is only given to those who have attained enough faith."* If the truth were to be known, in the innermost part of their being, people who rattle off such phrases are trying to tell themselves that they are excluded from suffering and death because they are more "spiritual" than most. In all actuality, these illusionists are just scared to death to die and are trying to convince themselves that they are exempt from the reality of the grave.

The opposite of the exclusive mind-set is an inclusive community approach to the problems of life. Those whose theology is inclusive acknowledge that faith-filled people continue to get sick and die every day all over the world. They realize that some people's deaths are simply more drawn-out and public than others and that we are all really in the same boat, on a journey to the grave. They understand that we're here on earth to help each other recover from personal shipwrecks. Those who have an inclusive perspective are realists, while people who choose to adopt the exclusive "faith" theology are deniers of the reality of our human predicament.

As reality Christians, it is important for us to consistently re-examine our beliefs and our understanding of faith in order to purify our theology. The twentieth century theologian Paul Tillich best describes this in his Protestant Principle that *every so often we should take our faith and hold it as if up to the light, re-examining it to look for new revelation. Otherwise, our faith has a tendency to atrophy.*

The Protestant Principle contains the divine and human protest against any absolute claim made for a relative reality, even if this claim is made by the church ... it is the guardian against the attempts of the finite and conditioned to usurp the place of the unconditional in thinking and acting. It is the prophetic judgment against religious pride, ecclesiastical arrogance and secular self sufficiency and their destructive consequences.

Tillich

When we become stubborn in our own pious convictions, we are in danger of missing the message of Jesus and misinterpreting biblical scriptures by isolating appealing verses to reinforce our own personal religious beliefs.[47] We are in danger of becoming illusionists who delude ourselves and others. To merely proclaim God's word concerning healing without the experience of being sick means to limit oneself to not really knowing God's word. In order to truly understand the plight of the afflicted, one must at times be a fellow traveler with those who endure living with physical frustrations. In other words, only those people who have "been there" should be the ones to address the issue of physical healing in religious settings. Otherwise, we are in danger of adopting an erroneous, exclusive, flawed faith theology instead of the accurate inclusive theology that we humans are all in the same boat in a turbulent world.

Those who proclaim that people who have *enough* faith will be excluded and exempt from disappointment, pain and suffering in life try to live constantly in what they perceive as the spiritual world. They attempt to become spiritual enough to be able to obtain blessings galore, perfection, and utopia in the temporal world on earth. (The gospel Bob Shervly proclaimed is prevalent in conservative Charismatic theology.) Some faith healers even claim that they are "little gods" who can control God and bring forth anything they desire by the power of their words.[48] This way of life does not include living in the realities of the world and excludes others who must, often leading to an arrogant pseudo spiritual life. The danger is that Christians who strive for heaven on earth — an earth without pain, without suffering, and without sickness — can become critical and judgmental because the concept of exclusivism doesn't allow them to listen to the cries of a hurting world; but instead they judge the world. This errant mentality focuses on a concept of being self-divine by professing to be able to coerce God while forgetting the realities of being human. Therefore, this concept becomes an illusion.

83

Bob Shervly is an illusionist with exclusive beliefs. He used Biblical texts out of context to blame Alan and Jan for having to deal realistically with problems in an unfair and imperfect world.

The positive alternative to this is to choose to participate in the inclusive community. In this realistic community, compassion and empathy have an opportunity to exist. When we choose to face life with an inclusive attitude, we are more likely to be a community that learns to serve one another, bear one another's burdens, understanding that we all live in a world that just isn't fair sometimes. The inclusive community doesn't deny the reality of disappointments and accepts the reality of pain in this world, yet, lives with an attitude of transcendence. (Above and beyond the limits of experience.) People who are involved in this community help others face their hurts and frustrations by standing beside the victims of the world; they do not want anyone to face the harsh realities of life alone. Participation in the inclusive community is not necessarily spiritual. The inclusive community cries together, accepting that suffering injustice is simply a part of the journey of life.

The inclusive community embraces the belief that Christ has two natures. His divine nature preaches hope for the day when there will be no more tears, no more sorrow, and no more death. His human nature tells us by example that it hurts to be human. Effective followers join together to bear the burdens of life between them. They strive toward standing alongside those who are victims without casting judgment. Victims can become victors in a supportive environment. The inclusive community is what Jesus asked us to participate in. Those who are involved in it are Christ's contemporary disciples. The inclusive community is earth-related, for it exists in the same flesh as that of Jesus of Nazareth, but it is not earth-bound for it lives in the same spirit, constantly looking toward the eternal.[49]

Let's continue examining these two different ways of living: learning to avoid negative, judgmental, exclusive beliefs and instead learning to live within the Christ-centered inclusive community as reality Christians. Let's first examine judgmental phrases that are commonly used toward persons who have experienced physical maladies and compare them to the judgment commonly served to people who are poor.

Judgment of the Oppressed	**Judgment of the Afflicted**
"Lazy"	"Not enough faith"
"Uneducated"	"Satan is in your life"
"Bums"	"Not straight with God"
"Want hand outs"	"Being punished"

Do you see the similarities of thought behind the judgments? They are pronouncements of opinions of a formal authoritative nature without any experience. How can the rich judge the poor? How can the healthy judge the sick? How can those who have never suffered judge those who must endure? Here we do not find wisdom or truth.

Judgment against those who suffer comes from an exclusive way of life, a life that is guilty of believing some people are exempt from pain and suffering because of their superior spirituality. Unfortunately, this is the trap that many charismatic denominations seem to fall into and is especially prevalent among those in the "word of faith" movement.[50] It stems from the American imperialistic mind-set of wanting to control and dominate. This approach to religion has a tendency to want to control God and God's response to us by expecting Him to give us whatever we demand because, somehow, we think we deserve His blessings. (As in chapter III, we think we deserve a lifetime supply of bread and fish.) It conceals this true desire by hiding behind the skirts of super-spiritualism and the using of such shibboleths as *"having*

85

enough faith." As we have previously discovered, according to this errant philosophy, a person can attain physical healing or any other desire from God by believing strongly enough that it will happen. This gives us an image of God that closely resembles a Santa Claus whom children write to and then receive gifts from on Christmas day. Only the good girls and boys who *really believe* in Santa receive the presents of their dreams. What if Santa exercises the freedom to give each child whatever toy he happens to pull out of his sack at the moment instead of giving the one a child has listed? What if, for example, a little girl asks for a doll house and instead Santa brings a box of materials for the child to build her own doll house? Christmas morning, we can imagine the child running into the living room expecting to find a beautiful doll house only to find in its place a pile of wood. The child, who had her heart set on a specific doll house, breaks into tears, feeling immediate disappointment. She has the choice to pout and say, *"I never really believed in Santa anyway,"* and throw away the stack of what seems to be useless wood saying, *"I wanted a toy. I didn't want to have to spend time building it. That's too hard and takes too much work. I wanted Santa to do all the work so I could play,"* or she could choose to creatively use the materials Santa left to build a doll house of her own unique design.

I see our lives as a stack of wood that was given to us the day we were born. We weren't allowed the option of choosing the kind of wood we wanted. Some were given plywood, others were given oak. None of us was presented with detailed instructions of how to put it all together. We were given the freedom to creatively build our own lives from the basic materials we were originally given. We have the choice to build or not to build. We have the choice to say with the child when we don't receive specifically what we ask for, *"I never really believed anyway,"* or *"I'm going to build a castle from this plywood."*

Those who possess an exclusive mind-set actually want to be little gods themselves. They constantly choose to eat the apple in the garden of Eden, so to speak. The facts are we are merely mortal and we can't control God or receive all we desire by merely believing *enough* or by saying the *right prayer* just as the child didn't receive the doll house she asked for even though she wrote a beautiful letter to Santa. We don't know why some people receive plywood and other people receive oak. We are not able to know complete specifics about the mind of God. If we were, then the mystery of God wouldn't be a mystery anymore and faith would be unnecessary.[51] If, however, we seriously try to understand the significance of the accounts of the life and death of Christ we can find comfort in believing that God is ultimately concerned with the eternal ramifications of all that transpires as we work on building our individual lives. Then we can find comfort in the hope that God will bring about justice, and that the Creator does care about hurting humanity.

> *"Theological arrogance needs to be corrected by reverent agnosticism. We need to remember that in the presence of God we are confronted by a meaningful mystery about which it is possible and appropriate for the Christian to speak with conviction but never with dogmatism ...we are able at best to "see through a glass darkly."* (1 Cor. 13:12, KJ)
>
> Tillich

To *"see through a glass darkly"* means that while on earth we are barely able to comprehend the heavenly. **God doesn't give some a clearer glass than others to look into.** Some people have a tendency to claim that if a person becomes spirit-filled he can experience things of the spirit in a dramatic way. Outlandish statements such as *"God told me to raise sixty million dollars to build this church"* and judgmental shibboleths that begin with such phrases as *"God revealed to me that..."* are indications of someone who is trying to claim that he or she has more spiritual insight than other Christians have. This all stems from desires to attain the knowledge that only God possesses and to acquire gifts from a

87

Santa Claus-type god. In a way, it is the constant tasting of the forbidden fruit.

Those who understand at best that we are only able to *"see through a glass darkly"* are the people who are involved in the inclusive community. People who are living in the inclusive community understand that we are all given different kinds of wood from which to build our lives. Some were given plywood, others oak. The inclusive community doesn't ask, *"Why was Robert given plywood?"* but instead helps each person build castles of purposeful living.

The inclusive community is courageous enough to *"Bear one another's burdens"* (Gal. 6:2). It lives in the world, yet not of the world (John 17:16). It understands that Jesus lived in the world, which included having to experience physical pain, God forsakeness, and death, and, therefore, gained compassion and true empathy for the world.

The inclusive community embraces the definition of Christ's humanity as *"a man of sorrows and familiar with suffering."* (Isaiah 53:3, NIV). It accepts the reality that Christ died and tries to encompass all of life's experiences:

> *"... so that Christ may dwell in your heart through faith;*
> *and that you, being rooted and grounded in love,*
> *may be able to comprehend with all the saints what is*
> *the breadth and the length and the height and the depth."*
> (Eph. 3: 17-18, NAS)

The inclusive community accepts pain and suffering as reality and participates in the faith of Jesus; therefore, it is united with the whole person of Christ. It embraces the fact that the cross is the argument against all idealism, and it is the symbol that the world continues to crucify the message of God's outreach and exaltation of the outcasts of the world.[52] The exclusive way of life denies the reality of sufferings; thus, it eliminates the choice of faith, for no person desires affliction. If all people could earn freedom from disease by attaining enough faith, there would be no choice but to serve God. The inclusive community embraces the reality of suffering and yet lives a life of transcendence—not avoidance.

The exclusive way of life is an end to itself. It desires visible changes and blessings here and now; therefore, it lives in the temporal. It ignores the reality of the cross and is blasphemous toward the crucified Christ. The inclusive community looks to the eternal and lives a flourishing, productive life in spite of all that contradicts a happy existence.[53] It is within this community that the individual can proclaim:

*"I am well content with weaknesses, with insults, with distresses,
with persecutions, with difficulties, for Christ's sake;
for when I am weak, then I am strong."*
(II Cor. 12:10, NAS)

To claim a life of blessing for those who *"have enough faith"* separates people from the realities of living in the world. The moment two or three attempt to embody the difference in any form that separates them from other people, a boundary has been drawn that will place Christ on one side or the other.[54] *Christ will* **always** *be on the side of the humbled person. Christ will always be on the side of the sick, the poor, the forgotten, the hurting, the ignored, the broken.* What side does that leave for the pious Christian living his "holy," exclusive way of life?

When the reality of suffering is denied, the message of Christ is completely ignored. If we only accept a gospel of blessings, we separate ourselves from the inclusive community and we deny our actual existence. Christ suffered with humanity. If the Son of man is not exempt from pain, then I am not exempt. Christ did not escape or deny suffering. He lived with humanity. He died with humanity. Jesus, as the divine liberator, condemned "ivory tower" Christian Pharisees such as Bob Shervely who know only partial truths, yet proclaim their own goodness. He praised those who endure all things. (I Cor. 4:12, II Tim. 2:3, Heb. 12:7, Pet, 2:20, Rev, 3:10)

Our goal as reality Christians who live in the inclusive community should be to grow from making "arm chair" judgments, commenting on subjects that we haven't experienced, and go into the examination hall of those who are suffering, bearing each other's burdens, trying to understand each other's pain. Only after sitting on the benches of the humbled will we be entitled to enter a school of higher learning.[55] With this education we begin to participate in the liberation of judgments and live realistically in our imperfect world. In other words, it's time to give up our childhood belief in a Santa Claus god who will give us whatever we ask for as long as we believe in him *enough.* It's time to grow up and admit there really is not a Santa Claus.

The religiosity of those who worship the Santa god does not include a willingness to face the realities of living in an imperfect world or the quality of humility. Those who adopt this exclusive mind-set proclaim their own superior spirituality and throw innocent victims into a faith hall of shame.[56]

You, however, understand what faith really is because if you have suffered in any area of life, you are fleshing out the faith journey every day of your life. Those who honestly follow the teachings of Christ face the problems of life realistically and humbly admit that the Jobs of the world are the heroes of faith. The historical documentation of the life of Jesus teaches us this. He suffered with humanity. He did not, in His divinity, escape or deny suffering. He lived with humanity within the inclusive community. His life was an example of how we should respond to injustice and to those who suffer in an unjust world.[57] I am responding by telling you that your walk through the valley of hard times is to be respected. You are a champion of faith. Carry on, my friend.

THE GARDEN

CHAPTER VII

The darkest hour is just before dawn.
Proverb

The Garden

"Let this cup pass from me"
(Matt.26:39)

"*Help God! I'm hurting! Please do something!*" Have you ever uttered similar words during a time in your life when you just didn't think you could handle any more disappointment or pain? Where can you go for guidance when life hurts? Is there anyone who can help? Perhaps …

Let's take a look at the suffering of Jesus as He prepared to face His death on the cross. The window we have been given to enlighten us is what I call Christ's garden moment. I am referring to Christ's time in the Garden of Gethsemane when He prayed to God, knowing that torturous sufferings lay ahead of Him and when He was aware that He would soon make the long journey to the cross where He would be physically beaten and tortured to death.

The Garden of Gethsemane

"Then Jesus came with them to a place called Gethsemane, and said to His disciples, 'Sit here while I go over there and pray.'
And He took with Him Peter and the two sons of Zebedee and began to be grieved and distressed.
Then He said to them, 'My soul is deeply grieved to the point of death; remain here and keep watch with me.'
And He went a little beyond them and fell on His face and prayed saying, 'Abba, if it is possible, let this cup pass from me; yet not as I will, but as thou will.'"

(Matt 26: 36-39, NAS)

Notice His plea to God to *"Let this cup pass from me."* In other words,

"Help! Help! Help! Stop the pain, intervene! Rescue me. I don't want to hurt. I don't want to have pain. I don't want to suffer. Help me. Please rescue me."

Do these words sound familiar? Have you ever pleaded with God to intervene and rescue you? If so, then you have had a garden moment. Maybe you have had several of them. I know I have. I remember pleading over and over with God to deliver me from the illness and from having to face major brain surgeries, to deliver me from having to endure extreme pain, suffering, and facing death.

"Don't let me go through this, God. Rescue me. Let this cup pass from me." This is the statement of our own personal request. It is what we want for our lives, a plea to save us from what we don't want. It is human nature to ask to be delivered from pain and suffering. Christ's plea demonstrates to us that part of the journey of faith includes calling out to God to rescue us from suffering. I must have prayed every day for God to rescue me. I begged and cried out, *"Help! help! help!"* I am convinced that even that cry alone helped me feel that somehow God was near. Why plead to be rescued if you don't believe anyone is listening? The cry of *"rescue me"* is, in itself, a cry of faith.

What happened next in the garden? What were Christ's next words?

"Yet, not my will, but yours be done."
(Matt. 26:39)

In other words, in resignation, Christ shrugged His shoulders and said, *"Whatever, God."* I believe that these words were said when Jesus had become too tired to pray anymore. I believe it was a cry of hopeless abandonment. Have you ever felt that way? Have

94

you ever reached the point where you were too exhausted to pray? Have you ever shrugged your shoulders and said to yourself, *"Why am I praying anyway? Nothing is answering. I don't even care anymore. Whatever, God"?* I know I have, and I believe that Jesus did in His garden moment. This insight into the garden makes Jesus' suffering all the more real and identifiable. It lets us know that part of the faith journey includes giving up on God sometimes and just saying in frustrated resignation, *"Whatever, God."*

> *"...we are heirs of God and co-heirs with Christ,*
> *if indeed we share in His sufferings*
> *in order that we may also share is His glory."*
> (Romans 8:17, NIV)

I believe that the true faith-filled person has had the experience at one time or another of being too fatigued to pray anymore. Does this imply that faith means we turn our back on God forever and give up on Him completely? No, of course not. This means that we can rest in the comfort that even God's Son knows what it's like to be too exhausted to pray. The fact is that experience is part of being human. It doesn't mean that you don't have enough faith. It is an indication that your faith is very big because deep down, in the innermost part of your soul, you are still trusting that God will see you through even when you are too tired to pray. This is what it means to sigh, *"Whatever, God,"*[58] in a garden moment.

I believe there is knowledge that can only be learned in a garden experience. It is the revelation of who God really is. When we learn to trust the One who created us, in spite of all that contradicts it, our faith becomes personal and we discover who we really are. It is in the garden experience that we are humbled before God. All our pretentiousness, our illusions of being in control of our lives, our arrogance, and egotism are exposed as ignorant vanity. It is here that we realize that *God is even bigger than our little prayers.* God knows the heart. We don't have to perform for Him. It is in the garden experiences of life, when we are too tired to pray anymore, that the unseen God becomes *"Abba."*

What does "Abba" mean? As we study the Scriptures we find that during Christ's moment in the garden, as He was pleading to God for divine intervention, He called God "Abba." What is the significance? It is important to note that the church leaders at that time spoke Hebrew, which was the elite language used to address God. God was usually referred to in what would translate as "The Lord" or "The Holy One." His name was uttered in respect for the God of all creation. It was the language of liturgy.

The word "Abba," however, is not Hebrew, but Aramaic — the language only used in the home and everyday life. Even in the Aramaic language, "Abba" is not a formal word, but is a small child's word that belongs only in the intimacies of the family circle. Scholars have said that "Abba" was an endearing name that a child would use to address a parent that he or she loved and trusted.

For an analogy, think of a small child who, at the end of a long day, crawls up into his parent's arms and says, *"I'm too tired to talk anymore. I'm too tired to walk. Carry me."* The parent then carries the child upstairs and puts him gently into bed. The child then rolls over and whispers, *"I'm too tired to say prayers tonight. You pray for me."* How would a loving parent respond? My guess would be that the parent would nod his head in understanding and let the exhausted child rest.

Using our knowledge of the word "Abba," I believe we can understand what this scripture means:

"Truly I say to you, unless you are converted and become like children, you shall not enter the kingdom of heaven. Whoever then humbles himself as a child, he is the greatest in the kingdom of heaven."

(Matt. 18:3, NAS)

When we let down our defenses, stop worrying about having to say the "right" prayer, lose our selfish pride and ambition, and realize that we really are not in total control of our lives, we become like children and can say "Abba" to God.

There are those people who will continue to insist that faith means to pray elaborate prayers until a specific request is granted. They may use judgmental shibboleths such as *"If you only had more faith..."* or *"I am praying for God to increase your faith."* What these dear people don't realize is that **you already have enough faith!** If you have experienced garden moments and are still choosing to believe in a good God anyway you are a champion of faith! To be a champion of faith is to live through a garden moment, understand that life hurts and is unfair sometimes, and still believe in a God of love *anyway.*

> "The location at which we say Abba to God always has something of Gethsemane about it; it is the place where the son comes home to the security of his Father's love and knows that he can trust it and all the provisions that it will make for him, but it is also the place where he is called and enabled for a new and costly obedience, where the way ahead is going to have in it something of death and something of glory, till at last there is final death and final glory. That is the inheritance of all God's children."[59]

Those who demand *"more faith"* from people who are suffering need to examine again what faith is. Faith, Christologically, is a faith of exhaustion, of endurance, a faith that believes *"in spite of"* temporarily unanswered prayers.

"For momentary, light affliction is producing for us an eternal weight of glory far beyond all comparison, while we look not at the things which are seen; but at the things which are not seen; for the things which are seen are temporal, but the things which are not seen are eternal."

(II Cor. 4:17-18, NAS)

Faith looks constantly to the eternal and believes that God understands when we can't pray anymore. This is the faith of the humbled. The person who has experienced a garden moment, when the words *"Whatever, God,"* are finally uttered in desperate resignation of even giving up on God, is the person who truly knows the meaning of the word *faith*.

Does this mean that it is okay to give up completely on God? No, a garden moment is just that, a moment. It is a time of frustration and resignation while we rest in the comfort that God understands our innermost being. Does the whispering of *"Whatever, God,"* mean that we should stop seeking physical healing when we are ill or that we shouldn't seek answers to our problems? Of course not! We all want to feel good. We all desire health. I believe that God grieves when His children suffer and that He wants us all to enjoy life. All knowledge and wisdom originates in the mind of the Maker. What is medical science but a form of wisdom? I believe that medical science is a tool God created for man to help those who are physically suffering find assistance, relief from pain and sometimes healing. Anything that helps to relieve suffering contains a glimpse of the goodness of God.

We were made in the image of the Creator of all that exists. We were made to be creative creatures — to hunger, to learn, to grow, to discover, to create. I believe it is a part of God's will for His people to search for creative solutions to problems, which include seeking physical and psychological help when needed. God doesn't want His children to suffer, and He applauds those who seek to help other people have a more comfortable existence.[60] God uses medical doctors to heal. I believe God uses people in practical ways to help other people. I encourage you to seek all the practical help you can find. I encourage you to tell God your desires, as Christ did when He said, *"Let this cup pass from me."* I encourage you to find a friend whom you trust and respect spiritually to pray with you. Present your requests to God. He cares about you. To say *"Whatever, God,"* is not to quit searching or to give up hope, but rather to acknowledge that part of faith is resting in the knowledge that God understands when you are hurting too much to pray and to ultimately realize that in your weaknesses you are a hero of faith.

"Therefore I am well content with weaknesses, with insults, with distresses, with persecutions, with difficulties for Christ's sake; for when I am weak, then I am strong."

(2 Cor. 12:10, NAS)

This is the faith journey as is presented to us in the book of Job. The inclusive community should, therefore, honor the journey of the person who is suffering and reprimand, with love, Job's friends when they start judging again and demanding *"more faith"* when they themselves may have very little.

The inclusive community can be recognized not by whom it judges and renounces, but by whom it is willing to receive.[61] The inclusive community can also redefine who the cripple is. Is the cripple the woman in the wheelchair who in her prayer closet proclaims, *"Though He slay me, I will trust Him"* (Job 13:15) and proceeds to live daily in visible, painful, humiliation, faithfully enduring, or is the cripple the individual who is unwilling to face the realities of living in an imperfect world and then harshly judges and condemns others who must?

We are told by Jesus that our lives will be less than perfect.

"In the world you will have tribulation, (suffering) but take courage; I have overcome the world."

(John 16:33, NAS)

The temporal reality is that there will be pain, sorrow, disease, and death in this world. No one has ever died of wellness, and mortality is running at 100%. That's one death per person. No one is the last few hundred years or so has permanently left this world alive! The fact is: We live to die! The eternal promise is that Christ has overcome the anguish of this world. He promises an eternity free of disease, pain, sorrow, and death.

Those who must endure living with physical challenges, disappointments, frustrations, and sorrow are the faith-filled believers. It's time to acknowledge the tremendous faith that many times goes unnoticed and is sometimes judged incorrectly as "a lack of faith." It is time to liberate people who are suffering from the burdens of judgment and public humiliation.

I believe the true church to be not the buildings nor the clergy, but the cries and the praises of the afflicted and the oppressed for God to have mercy. This does not exclude anyone, but embraces us all, for we are all afflicted and oppressed. Webster defines oppressed as *"persecuted, weighed down."* Who is not *"weighed down"* with the burdens of this world? Are you? I have been. The definition of affliction is *"one who is in pain, suffering, or is in great distress."* Who has not experienced *"great distress"* mentally, spiritually, emotionally, or physically at some time in their lives? Haven't you? I know I have.

We are all included in this faith-filled journey. All of humanity cries for liberation. The cry for a savior unites us. Christ is the mediator for those who have lived with burdens and for those who have observed those carrying the burdens. We should share every burden among us as an inclusive community, remembering that even the Son of Man was not exempt from suffering. If He was not exempt, then I am not exempt. None of us is.

"Often Christians have proclaimed a cheap grace that offers the forgiveness of the gospel without the discipleship demands of the gospel."[62]

We Christians accept the doctrine of Christ's atonement for our sins. We participate in the faith of Jesus. Shouldn't we also understand that part of the faith journey includes living in a world with serpents and stones, where bad things happen to good people?

100

"Therefore since Christ has suffered in the flesh, arm yourselves
also with the same purpose, because he who has suffered
in the flesh has ceased from sin."
(1Peter 4:1, NAS)

During my extensive time in the garden, I gradually began to understand that the inclusive community is what Christ's ministry was all about. He lived among the poor and sick, bearing the burdens of humanity. The humbled were Christ's everyday companions — those whom the world rejected, those whom the world considered "less than." [63]

I know that I had never understood the plight of those who suffer before I personally became one of those who is considered "less than." Almost overnight I became stigmatized. Life definitely looked different from a hospital bed than from a "Miss America" stage. Yet, it was there that I began to grasp the knowledge that can only be learned in humble despair and loneliness. With this knowledge we begin to identify with each other and to discover the meaning of the word faith.

THE NOTHING SPEAKS

CHAPTER VIII

God made everything out of nothing, but the nothing shows through.

Paul Valery

The Nothing Speaks

"My God, my God,
Why have you forsaken me?"
Matt. 27:46

On the twenty-fifth of February I was admitted to the hospital. Upon arrival, I was informed that I was to undergo a procedure called an angiogram before the surgery could be performed.

Once again I was told that I was facing possible paralysis and death with even this procedure. The doctors explained to me that the angiogram was necessary and, in fact, that they would not perform the surgery without it. The procedure would determine in which side of the brain my memory was stored. If indeed my memory was stored in the right temporal lobe, I would not be able to have the surgery.

The procedure, as was explained to me that morning, is called the WADA test.

The WADA test is a very important preoperative test for the patient being considered a candidate for epilepsy surgery. It combines the arteriogram, a special x-ray of the head, with the injection of a short-acting sleep medication. The test shows which half of the brain is responsible for speech and memory. By determining before surgery where these are located, the doctor can decrease the risk of damaging these functions as a result of surgery. During the test the patient is positioned on the x-ray table and the arteriogram catheter is inserted in the groin, through an artery and guided all the way to the brain. Once the catheter is in the correct position, x-ray dye is injected through the catheter into the blood vessels supplying the brain, and the x-rays are taken. A short-acting sleep medication is injected through the catheter into the large blood vessel supplying much of the blood flow to one half (right, then left) of the brain. Almost immediately on injection, this medication puts one-half of the brain to sleep and the other half will be tested.

When the dye was first injected I felt a slight sting. I had heard of people "seeing stars" when they received a sharp blow to the head, but I had not had that experience until then. I could feel the liquid flowing through my body to my brain, then I felt an onset of sudden pressure, and actually saw stars. The right side of my brain was blocked first. I was asked to hold my arms straight up in the air, and asked to name everyday objects such as a ball and pencil. Then I was asked to read a few flash cards. Easy enough! The left side of my brain was then filled with the medication, and I was asked to do the same simple tasks. I remember trying so hard to tell them the name of each object, knowing in my heart I should know what they were, but for the life of me I could not remember. The test was a wonderful success! It established the fact that the function of memory was stored in the left side of my brain. We knew then that I would not lose any memory function with the surgery. In fact, when this type of surgery is successful, the patient actually gains significant, measurable IQ points with the removal of the overactive brain cells. The only risks to face now were **death** and **being paralyzed!** What a relief?

I was returned to my room. Surgery would take place early the next morning and I felt fearful, yet excited at the same time. The end of this terrible chapter of my life was in sight, but what would its conclusion be? What did the future hold? I prayed silently that God would guide the surgeon's hand, knowing that I was looking straight into death's eyes. The surgeon would be within $1/32^{nd}$ of an inch of cutting a main blood vessel that would mean instant paralysis of the left side of my body or immediate death.

The restless night ended at the crack of dawn when a young orderly sharply knocked on my hospital door. It was time to go. While being wheeled to surgery, I remember looking up at the loving, familiar faces of my family. Then the doors loomed ahead where my family could go no further. The loving, familiar faces quickly changed into the cold, unfamiliar, expressionless faces of the surgical team. As I looked into their unfamiliar eyes, I thought to myself in a sudden panic,

"These people are strangers! I'm allowing a perfect stranger (at least I was hoping he was perfect) *to saw open my skull and take out a piece of my brain!"*

I waited for a moment, expecting to suddenly have a wave of peace come over me or a scripture randomly run through my mind or something, *anything* that would comfort me. I had somehow always believed that in our darkest, most terrifying moments God would reveal Himself somehow to comfort us. I had heard stories of people receiving the perfect scripture to help them in their moment of need. I waited and waited and waited and then … nothing. Nothing happened. I couldn't even think of one scripture, although I had memorized several throughout my life. *"Okay, God."* I reminded Him. *"This is it! This is my moment of total agony and fear … I'm waiting …"* Then … nothing … Undeniably nothing … God was completely silent.

I looked up into the surgeon's cold eyes. Here was a man who didn't know me, didn't love me. To him, I was just another skull. I glanced over to the tray of surgical tools and shuddered at the thought of what could happen with the smallest tremor, the slightest slip. *"God help me,"* I cried in silent desperation. The Nothing answered. In resignation I whispered the words under my breath, *"Whatever... God."* With those words, my fear, and the nothingness, I allowed the anesthesia mask to be placed over my face and went to sleep.

GRAVESIDE REFLECTIONS

CHAPTER IX

It takes a long time to understand nothing.

Edward Dahlberg

Graveside Reflections

"Please, somebody … help me. Please help me … PLEASE!"

I awoke in such excruciating pain that I could barely form the words. As I waited for an orderly… a nurse… someone… the light dawned on my pain-filled brain, *"I'm alive! I must be alive or I wouldn't be in so much pain! I'm alive … but, oh, how my head hurts!"*

Soon a lovely face stood above me, "Welcome back to life!" she said.

In a timid voice I asked, "Did everything go all right?"

She reassured me that it had, but told me that I would have to wait for the surgeon to explain the details. While waiting, I began to try to move each muscle, from the bottom of my toes to the top of my poor, stapled head. Everything seemed to be working, but oh, the pain!

A few minutes later, which seemed to me like an eternity, the surgeon appeared above me. How small and helpless I felt! How humbling it was to be so weak without being able to even lift my head up. As he looked down at me, he reassured me that everything had gone the way it should have.

"How much of my brain did you take out?" I asked not wanting to hear the answer.

"Oh, a piece a little bigger than an egg!" With those comforting words, he walked away.

After the immediate post-surgery danger had passed, I was wheeled out of ICU, presumably on a comfortable journey to my room. As the orderly turned the final corner to the safety of my room, he pushed my bed on wheels straight into the wall! I felt a jolt of horrendous pain, but at the same time, I noticed the expression on the poor man's face. I am sure at that moment, he felt worse that I did. (Actually, I doubt it.)

Finally I was helped onto my bed in my own room. The first person to walk in was my dear mother. Those who know me well would describe me as being just a little bit ornery. Brain surgery did not alter this part of my personality and I decided to make the most of a dramatic moment. I'm sure I was quite a sight with thirty-seven staples in my head, my hair filled with blood and my eyes almost swollen shut. The stage was set to have some fun.

Mother said, sweetly, "Hi honey!"

"Who are you?" I asked.

A horrified expression crossed her face as she said, "Teri, you know who I am. I am your mother!"

"No," I said. "You are not my mother, I do not know you!" I allowed this to go on for a minute or two for the dramatic effect and then said, "Got you, didn't I?"

You know, I thank God every day that my mother is a godly woman. She really had a right to slap me! But instead, being a bit of a prankster herself, she decided to get in on the hoax. My sister, Kim, was the next victim.

Mother was laughing so hard, with the relief that I was alert enough to joke a few hours after major brain surgery that she had tears in her eyes and had to bury her face in her hands so as not to let on. Kim, of course, thought she was crying in horror because I supposedly had no memory.

"Who are you?" I asked.

"Teri, I am your sister, Kim. We are best friends, remember?"

"No, I have never seen you before in my life!" I allowed a few moments to slip by for the drama of the moment, and then smiled. "That's to get you back for all the times you told on me when we were little."

My sister, thank the good Lord, is also a godly woman! Orneriness must run in our family because she wanted to continue the prank when we called the rest of our family back in Kansas. (If you can't joke after brain surgery, when can you?) We had our fill of playing and finally reassured everyone that I was just fine. I am happy to report everyone is still speaking to me!

As I said earlier, the pain was excruciating. Traditional pain medication was not used at this particular hospital because of insensitivity and negligence. One physician actually became angry with me because I was in pain. It never seemed to occur to him that the removal of that amount of brain tissue would cause swelling, which causes an incredible amount of discomfort. I begged for relief, only to overhear the head nurse say, "She will just have to suffer!"

Three painful days passed ever so slowly. Instead of becoming stronger with each passing day, I was growing weaker. Something was wrong. I began to run a fever and was becoming dehydrated. I had been unable to drink or eat anything for several days. (Pre-operatively the patient is not allowed to eat or drink). It was my family who caught the warning signs and knew that I could die if something were not done. The physicians on staff had ignored all of the signals of distress; so my husband and my father, who are both physicians, began to give the orders to save my life. Once again, I was near death's door, only this time accompanying the fear was horrible pain. I was going to die after all.

"YOU FAILED ME," I accused God.

The Nothing answered.

"You haven't been here at all, not one moment. You don't care do you? I've gone through two major brain surgeries and now you're going to let me die?"

The Nothing was deafening. As I waited for something ... *anything* ... my anger gradually melted into reflection.

"I'm going to die," I thought to myself, *"I am really going to die! This is it. The big moment. The final hour! Okay, I'm going to meet my Creator, silent, though He is. What will I have to show for the fact that I've lived on this earth 30 years? ... Oh, yes, ... wait a minute ... I was a beauty queen! Then ... oh, yes ... then, I was a television host ... oh, oh, and a singer!"*

While all of those things were good in and of themselves, they seemed to hold little meaning as I reflected upon them on my death bed.

"Oh God, I'm not finished yet. Don't let me die." I screamed silently. The Nothing yelled back.

My relationships with other people slowly passed through my mind. The love I had shared with my husband and daughter, the laughter I had shared with a few close friends, a precious moment with my sister raced through my mind as I stood beside her on her wedding day, the recollection of all the holidays we had spent at my parents' house, the memory of vacations in Colorado with my in-laws, some of life's most precious moments crossed my mind as I waited to die. The Nothing was still present, yet in remembering those moments with family and friends I felt a little comfort.

As I reflect upon those moments I believe that the presence of God is found in the unobvious, the subtle, the unassuming—in what appears to most as nothing at all. God's goodness was found in the cup of cold water that a sympathetic nurse gave to me. His

114

goodness was apparent when my sister laid a cool rag on my forehead to try to relieve some of the pain. I could see the compassion of God in the faces of my family as they cried with me in agony. Although at that time, in my pain, the Nothing was screaming as loudly as ever, I realize now as I recall those horrible hours that I was still being comforted in quiet ways. Was it possible that God was trying to communicate His care through the concern of those around me?

I believe that this is what Christ meant the Christian community to be. I realize now that I learned more about Christianity in that cold hospital room with the silent God than I had ever learned in the organized church. Christ never meant for His teachings to become cold doctrine. His church is in the lives of people, not in concrete buildings. His doctrine is one of love and compassion, not of judgment and denial of sufferings. His mercy is found in the love one human being has for another. His presence in found in the actions of the good Samaritans of the world.

It seems tragic that sometimes we never realize how precious life is until we are faced with our own grave. It's lamentable that we waste our lives chasing fraudulent dreams, vying for the "crown" gospel, never fully understanding until we are forced to, that life is about forming relationships, holding hands with humanity, crying together, laughing together, caring about one another. Only in relationships can lives be changed and hearts healed. We belong to each other. Life is a precious gift. Each day, each hour, each moment should not be taken for granted. Each day I ask myself, *"If I die today will I feel that my life was full of meaningful relationships with other people, or will I be caught chasing rhinestones that tarnish with time?"*

I know you're holding you breath, right now as you're reading these words in great anticipation, wondering ... *"did she live ... or die?"* To relieve your anxiety— I lived! My husband and father had saved my life and they'll never let me forget it either! The danger had passed and my fear had once again turned into

115

orneriness. My sister walked into the room wearing her brand new glasses, which were rather large in size.

"Hi, Owl Eyes." I teased.

"Oh, you must be feeling better!" she said. Never one to let someone get the best of her, she retorted, "What do you mean calling me 'Owl Eyes'? Who are you to talk, Zipperhead?"

My sister's lightheartedness helped me more than any pain medication could have. Laughter really is the best medicine.[64] Between the laughter and the I. V., my body was healing. Two days later I was sent home.

Where are you, Lord?

God, I find it difficult to believe in you.
You seem so distant;
I never hear your voice.
I never see your face.
People are suffering from hunger, homelessness and violence.
Where are you?
Others seem so certain about you, so sure;
What's wrong with me?
Are you near in the world of money and power?
Where are you in a world that doesn't love or care?
Sometimes it's easy to find you in the countryside.
In the rock-like strength of the mountain,
or in the peace of the valley.
You touch us with your presence.
But what about bad housing, concrete jungles, polluted air?
What about violence, murder, starvation, sickness?
Where are you, Lord, in a world,
Where babies die each day of malnutrition
and marriages flounder from houselessness?
I know there are moments when I have found your presence.
I think you are present when someone cares and helps:
There's a glimmer in the misery.
It's a touch of your love, a sign of your presence.
I expect you to be outside the world,
But you're right in it.
You're right in the thick of things.
You're among the starving.
Suffering with them and saving them.
You're among the homeless,
Neglected with them and consoling them.

117

You're within the broken marriage,
Hurting with them and healing them.
You are suffering, Lord, with those who suffer!
Not just observing it, but suffering;
Not just suffering, but courageously accepting it;
Not just accepting it, but transforming it;
Not just transforming it, but working to lessen it.
Can I believe that the glimmer in the misery is your light?
Your risen hope?
Your eternal promise?
Lord, I believe; help my unbelief.[65]

FAITH: FACING REALITY
WITH EAGLE COURAGE

CHAPTER X

*While I thought that I was learning how to live,
I have been learning how to die.*
Leonardo Da Vinci

Faith: Facing Reality
With Eagle Courage

*"If we were constantly conscious of our own impending death,
we would find the courage to step out from the mass
and be the individual we were created to be."*

returned home, spent a week in recovery, and then life
continued on as usual, except without seizures. After a year
of being seizure-free, the doctors gave me a clean bill of health. I
had been cured, and it was time to go on. This was perhaps the
greatest struggle of all. I had left for the hospital a former beauty
queen who was in need of surgery. I had returned home a sober
young woman, sorely aware of my own frailties, vulnerability, and
mortality. I was an entirely different person. My family especially
noticed some changes. One day my husband commented, *"You
seem so different. You're so serious, now. Everything has to have an
ultimate meaning to you. You've changed so much."* My reaction
was, *"How can a person have a life changing experience without it
changing her life?"* Life was different. I had experienced the very
thing that I spent my life ignoring. There is pain in this world. There
is unjust suffering. Personal death is a reality of life.

Preceding the illness, I had felt for the most part that I was
invincible. I believe that all of us do, to some degree. We live in a
world of denial, believing that agonizing situations only happen to
other people. Only *other* people get sick; only *other* people die. We
deny that we are vulnerable, that we are not really in control of our
lives and our future. We refuse to admit the fact that we are frail

human beings made of dust. We reject that our life on earth is temporary. We reject the grave reality of death. I could not do that any longer. I wasn't given the option. I had been to the edge of my own crypt. I couldn't put to rest the fact that I had experienced the reality of the black, vacuous chasm of death. I had visited my own grave, peered over the edge and into the abyss of the nothingness, and God had been totally silent. For the next few weeks I felt constantly fearful. I had joined the ranks of the experienced veterans in the war of life. I had been a soldier on the front line, in the battle of suffering. I understood, first hand, how horrendously painful life can be. If God had been completely silent during the worst that life gives, then how could I trust Him and believe that He would care for the rest of my life? How could I have faith in a God that had allowed so much suffering and did not offer any comfort in the dark, torturous night? How could I believe that He was a God who is truly interested in us as individuals? How can a person accept the tragedy of a pain-filled past and trust a God who didn't send comfort? How can one truly believe that there is a God who cares?

Yes, I had experienced some relief from the love of my family and friends, but as I reflected on the most painful moments in that cold room where death had walked so closely by, I realized that I still felt that God had abandoned me.

I had been reared to believe that God protects His children. I had been taught that God sends peace during the most horrible times in life to help His children get through them. I had heard stories of other people who had experienced some sort of "supernatural" comfort or insight during their torturous moments. I had heard of people who claimed to have a perfect scripture to suddenly run through their mind in their hour of need. Why hadn't I? I had prayed ... pleaded ... believed. Why hadn't God protected me, His child, from at least some of the horror? Okay, I could accept the fact that life isn't perfect and that no one is exempt from suffering, but what I couldn't accept was the fact that I had felt abandoned by

God. Why was the Nothing God's way of communicating with me? Why hadn't I been spared at least some of the extreme pain after surgery? Why had my life been threatened again after surgery? Why? Why? Why? I had enough faith to go through with the two surgeries. Why didn't God at least intervene after surgery and protect me from the things that went wrong that had threatened my life for the third time? When was enough, enough? I felt that God had somehow cheated me because I hadn't been spared anything, especially God-forsakenness. I had been left to face it all alone with the Nothing.

The cold reality of my own desolate grave haunted my every waking moment. The vacuous presence of the Nothing threatened to tear away everything that I had believed in. Peace of mind evaded me until I discovered that there was peace to be found with the acceptance that there was no peace to be found.[66] I began to understand that this is the real faith journey. Faith is being able to look realistically into the empty abyss of death,[67] accept the Nothing and say, *"Still, I believe."* [68]

How do we accept this definition of faith? I believe acceptance begins by facing the realities of our limited existence.[69] Most of us spend our lives avoiding facing the inevitable.

"It's not that I'm afraid to die.
It's just that I don't want to be there when it happens!"
                                                      Woody Allen

Death seems too dark, too final, too empty. We Christians talk a lot about how we have the gift of eternal life, yet, I believe we fear death as much as every other human being. *"What if it's not true?"* we all think to ourselves when we experience the presence of the Nothing. *"What if there really isn't an eternity?"* I believe that if we would be honest with ourselves, deep down, these questions plague us all. Where can we turn for comfort? Where can we go for answers?[70] Let's examine how Christ viewed the subject of

123

suffering, and life and death issues. I believe this is something very important for us to scrutinize in order to grow in faith and become more comfortable with the inevitable journey to the grave. This analysis will be instrumental in helping you find meaning in life. It will help you to see more clearly the "big picture" of how all the pieces of life can fit together to form a puzzle of purpose.

Let's begin by defining who Christ, the man, was on this earth. What kind of person was the Son of Man? In theological terms, the Christ who walked this earth is referred to as the "Christ of Humiliation." The Christ of the cross states:

> *"My kingdom is not of this world."*
> (John 18:36, NAS)

What did He mean by that statement? If we examine His life on earth, we'll begin to understand. Let's review:

Jesus was born in a humble manger because there was no room for Him in the inn. (Luke 2:7) He had hay for a blanket and animals sharing His cradle. His family was of modest means, with His father being a carpenter by trade. He spent His life living among the poor, the sick, and the outcasts of society. He never had a home of His own, and He traveled barefoot. His disciples were fishermen and outcasts. The organized church shunned Him. He died a painful, humiliating death on a cross, persecuted by the organized church and the government, and He was betrayed by His closest followers. Who was this man Jesus? He was an outcast. He was a king who became a humble servant. He did not reign in glory on this earth.

"He grew up before him like a tender shoot,
and like a root out of dry ground.
He had no beauty or majesty to attract us to him,
nothing in his appearance that we should desire him.
He was despised and rejected by men,
a man of sorrows, and familiar with suffering.
Like one from whom men hide their faces
He was despised, and we esteemed him not."

(Isa 53:2 -3, NIV)

His glory was a cross of wood and a crown of thorns. The Christ of the cross is the Lord who is the servant who:

". . .being found in appearance as a man,
He humbled himself and became obedient to death,
even death on a cross!"

(Phil. 2:8, NIV)

The Christ of humiliation is the Christ of earthly death. Do we as believers really accept the implications of this fact? I suggest that we do not. To accept the Christ of earthly death would mean that we would have to face the harsh realities of our existence. To follow this Christ is to face reality, but observe how far we have gone to try to deny the realities of life. If we were to examine the organized church throughout the centuries, we would see that it has spent much of its time arguing over details of doctrine, changing the "truths" of the church's beliefs every century, which has resulted in producing numerous different denominations. We would learn of the building of huge monasteries and carvings of elaborate altars that will, as many already have, perish in time. We would see that numerous wars, hangings, horrors, and bloodshed have all been done in the name of Christendom. We would witness lust for power in the papacy, claims of being "anointed by God for service" from television evangelists who are, this very day, being exposed all over the world for fraudulent ministries. Lust for power, greed,

125

exclusivism, warped values, still exist in the organized church today that Martin Luther so appropriately named as deeds of the Antichrist.[71]

Dietrich Bonhoeffer stated that the church is only the church when it exists for others.[72] What is the true church? I suggest it is the congregation of hurting people. This congregation includes all of humanity. Surprisingly enough, it includes even those who oppress other people because of their own religiosity. In the inner core of each person's being we are all hurting and crying out to an unseen God for reassurance that we as individuals are valuable to a creator. *"Is there really a God who cares?"* We all cry in the depths of our soul, *"Does my life matter?"*

Where can we go for answers? The true church can be found wherever hurting people are. These are the faith-filled believers. Jesus honored the journey of the faith-filled believer who was a victim of the circumstances of living in an unjust world. He was and still is the friend to the friendless, the hope of the hopeless. These were and are His chosen people. These survivors are the courageous ones. He honors the broken for their journey and reminds us that one day our upside-down world will be turned rightside-up.

"Many who are first will be last, and
many who are last will be first."
(Matt. 19:30, NIV)

"For everyone who exalts himself will be humbled
and he who humbles himself will be exalted."
(Luke 14:11, NIV)

"I, the Lord, have brought down the high tree, have exalted the low tree, have dried up the green tree, and have made the dry tree to flourish: I, the Lord, have spoken and have done it."

(Ezek. 17:24, NKJ)

These passages are very difficult for most of us to accept. If they were not, we would already be giving badges of honor to those who are oppressed, afflicted, broken hearted and to those who have endured. God calls those who endure blessed (James 5:11). Do we? No. Instead, we humans have the tendency to belittle our fellow man. We look for weaknesses in each other to try to make ourselves feel better. Many times we immediately discount a person, labeling him as less than valuable if he does not meet up to the image of perfection as portrayed to us by Hollywood in the movie and television industry. We who are involved in the organized church sometimes accept this fabrication and in a safe, veneer Christian state we whisper to ourselves that people who have disabilities are not *actually* secondary citizens, but *forces of circumstance* have made them secondary. Instead of valuing the walk of the faith-filled Jobs of today, the survivors are simply pitied.

This is the stigma that marks the victims and accounts for their victimization. It is an acquired stigma, a stigma of social rather than genetic origin. But it is a stigma and that is the fatal difference! What has not been fully realized is that *those who are stigmatized will be ahead of those who stigmatize* in the Kingdom of Heaven. That is the part of the right-side up vision that makes us uncomfortable. So instead of conforming to the ways of Jesus, we continue to ignore His example and exalt those the world exalts and merely pity those the world ignores.

As an example, I was recently in Washington DC at the American Academy of Religion convention where many of the top scholars of religion in America gathered to intellectually search together for God. After a long day of lectures, a theologian friend of mine and I decided to go to the nearest Baskin Robbins for ice

127

cream. Several others had the same idea, so the place was packed with theologians and pastors. Just as I was about to take the first bite of pumpkin ice cream the door swung open and in walked a man who was one of the most physically challenged persons I have ever seen. His skin was severely disfigured, perhaps from a fire, perhaps from leprosy. His left arm was a mere quivering stump and he had no tongue. Half of the theologians and pastors immediately looked away while the other half stared at this person as if he weren't quite human. Without thinking much about it, I quickly ran to his side, stuck my hand out and said simply, "Hi, I'm Teri, what's your name?" As my new friend turned to shake my hand, his smile spread from his mouth to his eyes. Because he had no tongue I couldn't understand the pronunciation of his name so I quickly pulled out my notebook and asked him to write it.

"My name is Jeff. It's nice to meet you, Teri. I'm from Pennsylvania. Where are you from?"

"Kansas."

"Oh, the Wizard of Oz country! I don't wish to hold you up, but could you help me order some ice cream?"

As we were placing his order a camaraderie quickly developed between us. Something as simple as ordering ice cream became terribly important. When I looked into his eyes I saw a glimpse of myself. I had experienced being misunderstood, being labeled, and shunned. I had experienced the humiliation of being treated as less than human by people who didn't understand, and in the simple gesture of ordering ice cream I was standing up for another person who had experienced the same frustrations. By his wounds, in a sense, I was healed. After we had ordered, received the ice cream, and begun to say our "good-byes," my new friend quickly scribbled something on my notebook. I looked down to read the words,

"Thank you for speaking to me. God bless you."

When I looked back up, I just caught a glimpse of his coat as he swiftly left in the darkness. I had learned more in five minutes of ordering ice cream than I had sitting through the lectures of the most brilliant contemporary theologians in America all weekend long. I had learned that we help heal each other by sharing our wounds with one another. I learned why Christ chose to live among the sick, the rejected, the misunderstood, and the despised instead of in the glory of the temple.

As I travel along on my journey of understanding the theology that I live my life by and preach for, I realize that I must first start by examining the plight of the suffering servant. There is a knowledge that can only be learned in humble despair and loneliness. It is here that we begin to grasp and define what faith and courage really are. Those who have experienced despair, loneliness, humiliation, agony, and doubt, and are still choosing to believe in a loving God, are courageously faith-filled people. This is where my theology begins, for it is the man of sorrows, the man of tears, the Christ of Humiliation that identifies with our humanity. When we honor Christ, we are honoring the most humble man who ever lived. Who has humbled himself? The children, the elderly, the oppressed, and the afflicted haven't any other choice, for they stand humble before God and man. These are the greatest. These are the faith-filled. These are the courageous. These are the heroes of faith! These are the people who already have within them what I call eagle courage.

Have you courage?

Not the courage before witnesses, but anchorite and eagle courage which not even a god any longer beholdeth? He has heart who knows fear, but vanquisheth it; who sees the abyss, but with pride. He who sees the abyss but with eagle eyes, he who with eagle talons grasps the abyss; he has courage.

Nietzsche

To be counted as one of those who has courage, one must first be daring enough to try to *"grasp the abyss."* What does it mean to "grasp the abyss"? The dictionary defines "abyss" as "An unfathomable chasm; a yawning gulf; An immeasurable profound depth or void. A bottomless pit." What is the bottomless pit? It is the immeasurable great space between our temporary existence and the promise of eternal life. In other words, the abyss is the nothingness we all experience, and ultimately, the abyss is our own death. Why is it immeasurable? Because who can grasp the gulf between life and death, between death and eternity? Most of the time we humans do not have to admit that the abyss even exists. We are comfortable living with the illusion that only *other* people get sick. Only *other* people die.

In the above quote Nietzsche mentions *"grasping the abyss with eagle talons."* What does this mean? How does one grasp with eagle talons?

Imagine for a moment that you are standing at the top of a great canyon unable to see the bottom. The edges of the cliff are made of foreboding, jagged rocks. The cliffs are bare of any trees or brush. All that there is, is scabrous stone.

Imagine a beautiful, majestic eagle perched on the outermost edge, grasping a craggy stone with his talons, peering down into the chasm that ends only in darkness. You would not dare to stand so close to the edge for you know of others who have fallen in and been covered by the nothingness. It is so dark and so threatening that you turn away, trying to forget that you ever saw it in the first place. You live close to it, but because you are afraid of falling into it you never actually get close enough to peer into it. Yet, *you know it's there* and that fact tears at you inwardly all your life.

The eagle is confident in his perch because he knows he can fly across the abyss. You admire his courage as he sits calmly on the edge, wishing you could peer so close and so confidently into the darkness. You feel conflict within yourself, for there is a constant battle knowing that it exists, yet, you're afraid to look too closely.

To have the courage of an eagle is to be a unconflicted person, able to accept the fact that the chasm exists (the pain of life and inevitable death) and able to live in spite of it and because of it, at the same time. Those with eagle courage live triumphantly in spite of the pain of life because of personal trust in the final victory of eternity.

On the other hand, to be a conflicted person, which most of us are, is to inwardly fight the inevitable, to run from death, to avoid the reality of existence. The avoider knows inwardly that death is imminent, yet constantly pushes down the thoughts and pretends it is not. This is the person who lives in fear, and indeed never really lives at all. He lives in fear of the chasm of *"what could happen"* or *"what might have happened."*

There is another sort of person. This person lives on the edge of the abyss, working on a way to cross over it, for on the other side is a lush, green valley where fear, pain, suffering, and death are banished. One day this person finishes building his bridge; this bridge took days, months, even years to construct and it took everything the person had to build it. Then the courageous one places his bridge firmly over the dark chasm and assuredly dances, yes, dances, across it while confidently peering into the bottomless pit below. *"I made it!"* the courageous one cries aloud, *"I'm a survivor! Follow me! There is life on the other side of the abyss. Don't be afraid,"* He shouts to the onlookers who are still too frightened to cross over. *"I made it across. You can too. Follow me!"* The most wonderful thing about this bridge is that it is permanent, and other people can now cross confidently over to the green valley on the bridge that one daring person built.

Who was this courageous person? Who was the One who built and crossed the bridge between life and death? Who was the One who viewed the world in an upside-down fashion, reminding us that death is life? Who was the One who built a bridge from brokenness to, once and for all, lead others across the vacuous chasm of death?

131

"In Him was life, and the life was the light of all people.
The light shines in the darkness, and the darkness did not
overcome it."

(John 1:4-5, NRS)

"This is indeed the will of my Father, that all who see the Son
and believe in him may have eternal life;
and I will raise them up on the last day."

(John 6:40, NRS)

Jesus said , "I am the resurrection and the life.
Those who believe in me, even though they die, will live,
and everyone who lives and believes in me will never die.
Do you believe this?"

(John 11:25 -26, NRS)

But we still stand on the other side of the chasm. We were not there to witness the courageous One dance across the bridge. We still see the nothingness of the foreboding abyss, and it is frightening to behold. Yet, we must believe. What is the alternative? Does this mean that to be courageous one does not have any fear? NO! We are human. We are all fearful of the abyss. It's important to understand that fear is the path of faith. It is normal and okay to be frightened, to doubt, to wonder if there really is anything beyond the abyss at all. Faith says, *"I'm scared. I'm not completely sure I believe in life after death, but I will try to believe anyway. I may not succeed in totally believing, but I will choose to try anyway."*

To grasp the Nothing means to accept the reality that although we may not feel God's presence, although we may not experience supernatural thoughts running randomly through our minds in our moment of need, although our prayers may go unanswered, still we choose to believe and trust an unseen God. This is faith. To grasp the abyss is to accept the reality that life is painful at times and that death is imminent. To attain mastery over the chasm is to lose all illusions of life, to realize the falseness, the deceptions, the mirage of a painless existence and to choose to believe that at one time 2,000 years ago, a bridge was built to make it all worthwhile.

To grasp with eagle talons is to understand that though this life is temporary, though the abyss is frightening to behold, there is hope. This hope enables us to admit that life is short and to dare to make a difference, to dare to have eagle courage and to soar above the fear and disappointments of our temporary existence. This is not to say that to have eagle courage means that fear does not exist in the individual, but rather that one with eagle courage can soar in spite of fear.

The eagle is the only bird who will bravely take off for flight when a raging storm approaches. All other birds run for cover. The eagle flies directly into the storm unafraid and undaunted. I use this as an example to illustrate how the strongest individuals are the ones who use the hell in their life as a launching pad toward heaven. They not only weather the storms of life, but actually begin their mission of finding meaning in life when the thunder of life's storms begins rumbling in the distance. Let the thunderstorms of your life be your launching pad toward creating a purpose.

Storms will come in every person's life. None of us is exempt.

"It rains on the righteous and the unrighteous."
(Matt. 5:45)

Just because I survived one major storm doesn't mean that I am now exempt from facing another. The next time, though, I hope I'm better prepared. To be better prepared for possible storms and to heal from previous storms, we must remember that although the winds will blow and the rain will fall, *we have a choice* of what to do when the storms of life rage on. We have the choice to be bitter and to blame or to face the storms of life with eagle courage and gain through pain.

The eagle is also the only bird that understands the currents of the wind. All other birds flap their wings as fast as they can to take off for flight. The eagle merely waits patiently on its perch for the right current, and then it simply spreads its wings, allowing the wind to support its flight without effort. It is the only bird that truly soars. In other words, people who learn to face death realistically, learn how to live in freedom that will result in being able to view the world as if in flight, trying to always see the world in one piece as would a giant. It takes courage to view life in this way. Most people instead, turn their nose where they don't want to look, narrow their field of vision, and bite off the world in small manageable pieces like a beaver does.

This is what happens all too often in our organized churches. To *"bite off the world in small manageable pieces like a beaver does,"* is to spend our lives focusing on little things like arguing over doctrine, or dwelling on the favored sin of the decade.[73] (I do not believe that we should ever verbally attack anyone for his or her "sins," for we should take no pleasure in the faults of any person, since we were told to be very conscious of the beams in our own eyes.) A person who spends his life engaged in beaver mentality cannot be called courageous, and his faith is very small, for he does not face life realistically and never comprehends that those who must endure hardships on the earth are the champions of faith.

So what is faith? You should know, for you have faith! You who have suffered in any area of life and are still choosing to search and to believe in a loving God know faith well! You are already in the process of living the faith journey!

> *"I am now rejoicing in my sufferings for your sake,*
> *and in my flesh I am completing what is lacking*
> *in Christ's afflictions for the sake of His body,*
> *that is, the church."*
>
> (Col. 1:24, NRS)

You understand because you have lived through the dark valleys of life that the walk of faith includes God-forsakeness. It includes becoming at peace with the Nothing that we all experience. It includes believing when not seeing, *"Blessed are those who see and believe but more blessed are they who do not see yet still believe"* (John 20:29) Faith is choosing to continue believing in a loving God even when He doesn't send comfort in the darkest hours of life. *"We live by faith not by sight."* (II Cor. 5:6-7) Faith accepts that there is unjust suffering in this world. Faith says with Job, *"though He slay me I will trust Him."* (Job 13:15) Faith constantly views the world in an upside-down fashion, seeing those who are exalted in this world humbled and those who have lived a life of humiliation, exalted. The faithful understand who the heroes of faith really are. Faith includes experiencing the realities of pain, suffering, disappointments, and God-forsakenness, and saying, *"Still, I believe."*

AND THIS IS FAITH

I see a tear stained face,
crying out for grace,
but none is seen.

I hear an orphan's prayer,
asking for someone to care,
but all that is revealed,
is the loneliness he feels.

I know a heart that's breaking
desperate with uncertainty,
but silence is the answer,
Yet, they say, "Still I believe."

I hold a patient's hand
who does not understand
why there is pain,

Yet, in her agony,
she tells me why she still believes
that God is good and life is fine
and death is only gain.

I bow my head in sorrow,
thinking of God's precious Son,
and of those painful words,
"Not my will, but yours be done."

And this is faith
assurance in the heart
without seeing grace
though a prayer is offered up
a thousand times
the silence still remains,

My heart cries out for answers,
but only one is clear,
that faith is found in those
who still trust in God
through the tears.

There is one who's gone before us
the way of sorrow and shame.
He walked the road of suffering
and pain

And though He had the power
to heal His broken body
He turned away.
And this is faith.

—Kim Karr Noller

NOW WHAT?
VICTIM OR VICTOR

CHAPTER XI

Life can only be understood backwards,
but it must be lived forwards.

Kierkegaard

Now What? Victim or Victor

Most likely, the pain that you have had to endure has been intensified by other people who have judged you, misunderstood you, or even spiritually abused you. You didn't deserve to be treated the way you were in hurtful situations. People say horrendous things sometimes. People may have used judgmental shibboleths against you. It's time to heal the bitterness of the injustice you have had to endure that rages within you. To forgive and forget what another person has done to you is actually for your own benefit, to heal your own wounds. Try to accept people who have hurt you for who they are, recognizing that they are merely individuals trying to survive in a hostile world as we all are. People simply choose different ways to survive. Spiritual abusers survive by avoiding facing their own fears by trying to control God and other people. The exceptionalist attempts to blame victims because, in his own mind, it exempts him from suffering. People who cast insults at you are usually insecure people who gain self-esteem by separating themselves from others and by choosing to be prejudiced against anyone "different" from themselves. I am not trying to justify the actions of the people who have hurt you. I am merely stating that *for your own sake, for your own benefit and happiness,* it's important to choose to value the person who has hurt you and forgive the act of injustice. Becoming bitter won't hurt them, but it will hurt you. Forgiving the unjust act and valuing the person who was guilty of performing it will diminish having to live with the stress of resentment and the burden of hate in your life. The act of forgiving will enable you to be happier, and it just might help the person who hurt you, too.

You did not deserve the pain that you have had to endure in your lifetime, but whatever it is that hurt you happened. That's a fact we can't change, but now I ask you, what *are you going to do with it?* You and I have the choice of gaining through pain or spending the rest of our lives bitterly hurting. Are you going to choose to be a Victim or a Victor? It is completely your decision. Tim Hansel says, "Pain is inevitable; misery is optional." Don Juan once suggested that to the ordinary man, everything that happens to him is either a curse or a blessing. To a warrior, each battle is a challenge. Choose to challenge yourself to be a warrior. I encourage you not to spend the rest of your life as a Victim. I challenge you to take the path less traveled and choose to be a Victor.

> *Do not go where the path may lead.*
> *Go instead where there is no path and leave a trail.*
> Ralph Waldo Emerson

Only Victors can leave a trail for others to follow. Only Victors choose to create a purpose for the hurtful things that have happened to them. Only Victors win in the game of life.[74] Only Victors are brave enough to run past the base of bitterness and on to creating a purpose for the purposeless.

> *Progress always involves risk; you can't steal second base*
> *and keep your foot on first.*
> Frederick Wilcox

Part of learning how to be a Victor is allowing ourselves to open our minds to a large definition of God. I must say that because of my own post-personal holocaust knowledge, my childhood image of God is gone forever. In the words of James Kavanaugh, *"I have lost my easy god."*[75] I have lost the god who would protect me because of my righteousness. I have lost the sanguine god who seemed to be predictable and manageable. I have lost the god who smothered me with the "have tos" of religion. Instead, in the place of my childhood god, I have gained the understanding that God is a God of mystery. I have gained freedom in the knowledge that God is not a God of rules who only blesses the faithful, but a God of love who in absence is always present. I have gained a new understanding of what it means to serve a God who chooses to suffer with us. The Crucified Christ has become the center of my theology and the foundation on which I build my belief that unjust suffering can be used divinely if we as individuals choose to create a purpose for our pain. My knowledge of God is much more complex than before the holocaust, more beautiful and awesome. I believe I am one step closer to my understanding of who God is because of the holocaust. An easy God is easy to find; a hard God is hard to find. Many people completely lose all faith in God after the experience of suffering. This happens because people largely worship a small god. In order to maintain a belief in a loving God after a holocaust experience, one must begin to accept the mystery of a God who would choose to die on a cross as a religious criminal. The truth of God transcends organized religion and all small sanguine definitions of who God is. The truth of God is found beyond the experience of the Nothing.

A question I would continue to ask myself after my recovery was *"Is there something beyond the Nothing?"* To give you some comfort and hope, I will say that I would not have written this book if I believed that there were not. I do believe there is something beyond the experience of the Nothing, and I'll tell you why.

A short while after I had received a clean bill of health, I attended a conference in Canada to work toward finishing a Master's degree. After classes had adjourned for the day, I decided to drive around town to get better acquainted with my surroundings. One of the first places that I chose to visit was a little Jewish bookstore in the downtown area. I soon discovered that the owners of the store, Mara and Judith, were Holocaust survivors. As we began to share stories, Mara pointed to the Star of Daivd pendant that I always wear around my neck and asked me, *"Why do you a Christian American wear the symbol of our Jewish faith?"* I told them about my experience of having a portion of my brain removed without having the benefit of any pain medication during my entire recovery process and how that encounter of suffering gave me a soulful kinship with the victims of the Holocaust who were diabolically experimented on by the Nazi "doctors." The infamous Nazi butcher surgeons performed bizarre surgeries on innocent people without the use of anesthesia. Many of them were brain surgeries in which portions of the brain of their victims were removed so that the barbaric doctors could just see what would happen. Some of the connections in the brain were stumbled upon by these butchers, and what they learned at that time indirectly led to some neurological understanding that is used in neurosurgery today. I further explained to them that because I had lived through my own experience of anguish, I am determined to create a good out of the evil that I encountered for my own sake and in memory of the courageous people who died on those operating tables in the Holocaust.

Mara's eyes echoed the understanding that only one who has suffered greatly can possess. *"You are the good,"* she whispered in gentle recognition. I was taken back a little, not quite understanding what she meant, *"What do you mean?"* I asked. Mara leaned over and looked intently into my eyes. *"We believe that God's goodness will always, ultimately transcend all the bad in the world. We are ceaselessly searching to find a glimpse of God's love and in your story I see a glimpse. You see, we had a friend who was a victim of the cruel experimentation. She suffered permanent damage. We have always said to ourselves that someday God would redeem Himself. Someday we would witness His goodness transcending the senseless evil and you are giving us a glimpse that honors her memory. This is the way He speaks in the silence. He speaks through the lives of people who faithfully continue loving Him and continue searching for ways to help other people in spite of not having their own prayers answered."*

142

Does this mean that it was God's plan for the victims of the Holocaust to go through all the horror, pain, and suffering at the hands of fiends like the butcher surgeons just so neurosurgeons would be able to better understand pathways of the brain that would eventually help people like me? Does this mean that God had planned since the day I was conceived for me to develop epilepsy, go through two brain surgeries without pain medicine so that a greater good could come out of it someday? Does this mean that it was God's plan for you to go through the valley of the shadow of suffering for some unknown future good? Am I saying that all suffering and evil has some abstract divine purpose and that certain people are directly chosen to fulfill that purpose?

No! To say that is cruel and heartless. That type of rationalization is the lighting bolt mentality we discussed earlier. The all too prevalent misguided belief that pain and suffering has a hypothetical, spiritual purpose that will be revealed when a good results out of monstrosity is cruel and disrespectful to human beings who have been victims of horrendous tragedies. I do believe that one way to show respect and to honor the lives of those who have been victims of cold-blooded evil is to create a good in humble reverence of their courage. Because of this belief, I am determined that somehow, some way, I will use the purposeless, traumatic experiences of my own life to help make existence easier for someone else who is facing a hellish time in life.

Through Mara's gentle words, I began to believe again that there is truly something beyond the experience of the Nothing. The something beyond the experience of nothing answering when we pray is called hope. Hope itself is the miracle that will help you survive a dark night of the soul. Hope is what will lead you toward finding a way that the senseless tragedies of your life can be changed into a triumph. Where does hope originate? From the same source love comes from, my friend. Hope and love all emanate from our Creator. The love of God is still there and can be found in the subtle wonder of the fact that goodness can be created from

143

the most intense injustice and horrendous suffering. God is not found in the glitter of the signs and wonders religion or in the *theologia gloriae* of the institutional church, but in the inaudible whisper of *"I still care"* when person discovers that she can help create something good in spite of meaningless, unjust suffering.

God's love will ultimately exceed all the horror and all of the pain that humanity has had to endure over the centuries. God's goodness will ultimately transcend all of the purposeless, horrendous suffering. Hold on to this hope, which is a glimpse in and of itself. Hold on with expectation that there is something beyond the experience of the Nothing and believe in your innermost being though circumstances may shout against you that God's goodness will ultimately shine through. Months, years, lifetimes may pass before a glimpse of goodness faintly flickers or a reminder of God's love is seen, but choose to believe that eventually goodness will surpass all suffering and pain. *"I'm still here. I still care,"* is the whisper of God.

If you are in the middle of a personal holocaust right now, then you are the one who needs to be ministered to by someone else who has suffered before you. Rest in this knowledge. Understand that you already have *"enough faith."* You do not need to somehow gain any more. You are currently a living testimony of faith and a hero in the community of those who follow the teachings of Jesus. Most people look for faith in the wrong places. Most people expect a person with faith to shout of victory over all of life's problems. Most think that faith is found in the lives of those who live in prosperity and health, but faith is found in the lives of people who live with scraping sores; not only in the lives of those who are surrounded by friends and family, but in those who are lonely and alone. Faith lives in the land of not yet and maybe never, of waiting, of not knowing, of uncertainty, and of doubt.[76] True faith is found in the home of the cancer victim, in the hospital room of the dying patient, in the lives of those who are well acquainted with the experience of the Nothing. Those who endure are the heroes. They know what faith really is. You know what faith truly is! Rest peacefully in the understanding that you are a champion of faith.

If you are a person whose personal holocaust is now a memory, then you can use your past pain to give others a glimpse of God's goodness and pass the baton on to the next runner. How can you aid God in creating something good from what you have endured in order to help give others a glimpse of the goodness of God? The first step is to make the decision to be a Victor rather than a Victim. The difference between being a Victim or a Victor is revealed by examining this question: *Do you have your pain or does your pain have you?* The Bible tells us that we all will have our share of favorable times and adversity in our lifetime. Not one of us will escape experiencing some rain in our lives. But we do have a choice of what to do with the rain when it pours. Are we going to wilt beneath the pressure of the pellets as the rain beats down, or are we going to allow the rain to sink down to our thirsty roots to nourish our soul, enabling us to grow stronger and taller, in order for us to bear fruit? We have that choice. You have that choice.

Is the fruit you are reaping today bitter or sweet? Bitterness is an easy monster to recognize. He doesn't hide his ugly face well. I can see him almost immediately in someone's eyes. He almost screams out, *"I am here. I own this body!"* As a baby the monster is called resentment. In his childhood he is called blame. As a teenager, the monster is big enough to own the facial expressions of its victim: curled lips, hardened eyes, and frowning brow. Once the bitterness monster is fully grown, nothing is ever its fault. It calls itself *"unlucky"* and despises the *"unfair"* world it lives in. Its favorite words are *"I can't"* and *"I won't."*

On the other hand, the most radiant people I know are not people who haven't suffered. They are people who have suffered greatly and found their freedom and joy in helping others. A person acquainted with creating purpose has a soft, yet excited expression in her eyes. Purpose is a soul-freeing angel of mercy. He is kind and just, loving, forgiving, compassionate, and joyful. He fills the

145

believer who allows him into her life with fulfillment beyond compare.

Why do I want you to create something good and meaningful from your pain? There are two reasons:

1) Your happiness

2) The world's benefit.

Do I really mean the world's benefit? Yes, I do. You have the potential to be one of the most inspirational people in the world. If you help just one person see a glimpse of the goodness of God beyond his pain, then you will be one of the most inspirational people in the world today. We will examine this fact shortly, but first, let's look at how creating purpose for your pain will bring you happiness. To do this we will compare the lives of two individuals who have suffered in their lifetime. One created a purpose. The other wallowed in bitterness. Both suffered humanly. Only one reacted divinely.

Mark

The first time people meet Mark, they immediately like him. His eyes are full of life and compassion. He is the first to ask, *"How are you?"* and if the reply is brief he will ask, *"How are you, really?"* He always hesitates to talk about himself, but on rare occasions he will reveal a little about his life.

"As a child I had severe asthma. I was limited in athletics because of the illness and sometimes felt alone and misunderstood. I was taken to see doctor after doctor and felt as though I was a problem to them. I would be rushed in and out of most offices and usually felt apologetic for having an illness. The drug I had to take to control the asthma stunted my growth and caused me to suffer problems with my complexion. My peers in jr. high school actually gave me the distinguished award of voting me 'the ugliest kid in the school.' I was institutionalized between the ages of thirteen and fifteen because of the severity of the illness. At that time I met one compassionate doctor who told me that he would teach me more about asthma than most doctors know so that I would feel that I had some control in dealing with my problem. He was true to his word and it made a difference in my life. I know, from experience, that ONE PERSON CAN MAKE A DIFFERENCE in the life of another. It was during those difficult years that I decided I would like to be a physician someday. I knew only too well what it felt like to be the patient; so I was determined to become a physician who would give each patient the gift of time."

Mark Spitz, M.D. is now head of the Epilepsy Center at University Hospital in Denver, Colorado. He is one of the most well respected neurologists in the nation. He spends, on the average, at least one hour with each patient, allowing the patients, *"as much time as they need so that they feel completely informed and relieved when they leave my office."*

Dan

Now, let's get acquainted with Dan. Dan is a twenty-nine-year-old man who proudly wears a tattoo of a snake on his arm and a bitter sour expression on his face. He is always the first to tell you how unfair life has been to him and how he *"could have been somebody if only God hadn't given him such a raw deal."* He will go on to tell you that he doesn't have a job because, *"I ain't gonna let nobody tell me what I can and can't do."* Dan's heartache began as a child. He explains,

"I wasn't ever given a fair shot. I was always smaller than the other guys and had this here problem where I'd wheeze and choke a lot, all the time. Them doctor's would make me take pills and stuff, but nobody's ever told me what to do, so I didn't take 'em too much. The other guys made fun of me cause I couldn't run fast and play on the team. I'd be somebody if God wouldn't have made me different like that."

147

Both men suffered as children. Bitterness has set its ugly teeth deep into one's heart. Compassion and empathy rule the heart of the other. Neither was given the choice of a healthy childhood. Both were given a choice of how to live their lives. One chose to be bitter and to blame; the other chose to create a purpose for his pain. Which choice will you make?

Humankind was created with the desire to have a purpose in life. Think about it. Why do so many people suffer from feelings of worthlessness and depression? Physicians agree that depression usually results when a person cannot find a purpose for living. We were created with the in-born desire to be needed, to be worthwhile, to make a difference in this world. To live happy, fulfilling lives means to live purposefully. Our society teaches us that we will have meaningful lives only if we are obviously, outwardly successful individuals who live glamorous lives as portrayed by the movie/television industry as the norm. I refuse to accept society's insistence that success comes only in obvious ways. Instead, I believe, as Erma Bombeck once said, that we can define *fame as Madonna, and success as Helen Keller.*

To live a successful life is to live a life of lasting purpose. To live a life of purpose is to embrace all of life to its fullest. This doesn't mean that you have to be a Helen Keller, a Billy Graham, or even a beauty queen. Living a purposeful life includes relishing in the simple joys of life such as enjoying the miracle of the laughter of a child, the beauty of sunset on a cool October day, or the feeling of holding the hand of someone you love. To embrace life and value the lives of those around you is to live purposefully; this will fill your life with moments of joy and will keep you open to possibly witnessing a glimpse of the goodness of God. Whether your life is a happy, joy-filled, purposeful one or not depends on how you choose to react to what life gives you.

Your Happiness

Ever since I chose to *"grow through"* suffering rather than become bitter because of the experience, I have met and counseled several individuals who have greatly suffered. I have learned that every person in this world has a cross of some kind to bear. Some allow their pain to crucify them. Others turn their crosses into bridges. Within a very short time after meeting a person, I can tell who wants to wallow in bitterness and anger and who wants to create a purpose for the purposeless pain they have had to endure. It is obvious to see who rules the heart by what's in the eyes. It is crucial to understand that how we react eventually determines who we become. How we react to suffering, disappointments, and frustrations is a choice all of us have to make. Whenever I meet Victors, I always ask them *"What has made you a Victor rather than a Victim?"* One of the most helpful responses I have received was from the man I introduced you to in the first illustration. He has chosen to gain through his pain.

When I asked Dr. Spitz how to become a Victor rather than a Victim, he said:

> "Victors always look for tomorrow, believing that tomorrow will be brighter than today. Victors see life as a challenge rather than as a drudgery. Victors change their expectations of life and include the reality of disappointment and frustrations in life's agenda. Victors choose, day by day, moment by moment to be positive no matter how many negatives are invading their lives. Being a Victor rather than a Victim is purely a choice on the part of the individual."

Who you are is a direct result of how you have chosen to deal with what has happened to you.

The World's Benefit

I believe that you have chosen to be a Victor rather than a Victim. Because of this very fact, you have the potential within you to become one of the most inspirational people in this world! How do I know this about you? I am sure of this because you are searching to create a purpose for the pain you have suffered in your life. This desire is very rare. Why is it so rare? It is human nature to wallow in self-pity and bitterness when the world is unfair. In fact, the easiest way to deal with the scars life gives us is to center all our thoughts and emotions on ourselves.

"Poor me. I would be somebody, but I was never given a chance at life. No one has ever suffered like I have. Why me?"

The easy way is the way most traveled. It is also, sadly, the most destructive and meaningless. But you are different! You are searching. You have great potential. Why? Because you have a desire to help and because you know pain. Think about it. From whom do you receive the most comfort? Usually, I have found that comfort comes from someone who knows your pain because he or she has lived it! You are someone's greatest comfort. You may be the only person in this world who can reach and revive someone who is, at this very moment, walking along the road you've traveled.

From talking with many individuals who have suffered great pain, I have learned that the common feeling each person shares is the despair of aloneness. You may be the only person who can break through that wall of isolation. You have something so valuable to give. There is no one as valuable and comforting to a person who is suffering as one who can actually say:

"I know what you are going through. I've lived it. I've been where you are."

Just look at how unique and special you are!

We also have the choice to not only survive *in spite* of the pain and injustice we've suffered, but *because* of it. To survive because

150

of the suffering you've endured is to creatively use the negative aspects of your life and change what seems to be a tragedy into a triumph. To create a purpose, one must always begin by looking at life from the perspective of an eagle in flight, always looking at the "big picture" and asking, *"How can this relate to eternity?"*

"Do not store up for yourselves treasures on earth, where moth and rust consume, and where thieves break in and steal; but store up for yourselves treasures in heaven, where neither moth nor rust consumes and where thieves do not break in and steal. For where your treasure is, there your heart will be also."
(Matthew 6:19-21, NRSV)

This scripture tells us that part of our purpose in life is to work harder than building the obvious. Our world demands obvious works before it will proclaim that a person's life is worthwhile. It's important to understand that we will usually find God working in the unobvious. We are asked to live with an attitude of humility, always looking for what would help make another person's journey on earth a little easier. This includes bringing cups of cold water daily.

"Whoever gives even a cup of cold water to one of these little ones in the name of a disciple—truly I tell you, none of these will lose their reward."
(Matt. 10:42, NRSV)

I interpret this scripture to mean that the little things we do daily are important and are what we are asked to do in the name of Christ, even if it is as small as giving someone a cup of cold water. "A cup of cold water" could be a phone call or a short note to someone who is hurting. It can be as simple as a smile and a sincere, *"How are you?"* It could be a hug or an *"I love you. I appreciate you. You're a terrific person."* A cup of cold water can go a long way in changing someone's day. These small tasks will usually go unnoticed, but they are very important in the eternal perspective. In order to be able to be sensitive to the needs of others, a person must be able to understand what it feels like to be in need. This is where your personal suffering experience enters in and where purpose for pain can be created.

YOUR CROSS—A BRIDGE, YOUR LIFE— A SYMPHONY.

CHAPTER XII

Life is either a daring adventure or nothing.
Helen Keller

Your Cross—A Bridge,
Your Life— A Symphony

*L*et's begin helping you create something of meaning and value from your pain by using the analogy of the civic center again, only this time the civic center is going to represent your life.

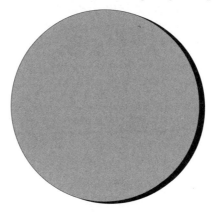

YOUR LIFE

Concert Hall I, where the symphony is always playing, is the majority of your life that is or has been good.

Concert Hall II represents whatever pain you have had to endure that disrupts the rest of your life.

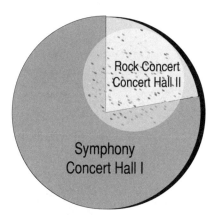

Concert Hall II represents the area of your life that, when used for good, will give the cup of cold water that no one else can give — a cup that might even save another person's life. It is the scar in your life that you can use to help heal another person's pain, and in that interaction a glimpse of God's goodness beyond the suffering can be detected.

It's true. You did not deserve the pain that you have had to endure, but it happened. Now I encourage you to ask yourself, *"What am I going to do with it?"* I challenge you to say to yourself, *"I can help someone because of my pain."*

"Suffering is overcome by suffering, and wounds are healed by wounds. For the suffering in suffering is the lack of love, and the wounds in wounds are the abandonment, and the powerlessness in pain is unbelief. And, therefore, the suffering of abandonment is overcome by the suffering of love, which is not afraid of what is sick and ugly, but accepts it and takes it to itself in order to heal it." [77]

A real life example follows: you know by now that the Concert Hall II in my life was having to deal with adult-onset-epilepsy that had resulted from a car accident seven years previously. Included in that concert hall was having to face my own mortality at a young age, which resulted in a desire to theologically search for "new truths" that would sustain me since the "old truths" did not. As I began my search, I realized that most people who have had any pain in their lives at all ask many of the same questions I was asking. My long and torturous search resulted in not only helping me find some sustaining truths, but also in helping others as I have shared these partial answers with them.

Another problem that I faced shortly after surgery was discovering the fact that no one had ever studied the physiological healing process of the brain after this particular procedure. The only research that was being done was the study of the psychological trauma, which is totally ineffective toward recovery if the patient or the doctor doesn't understand that the post-surgery healing process and trauma is primarily physiological and will resolve itself completely as the brain heals and reorganizes itself. Interestingly enough, patients who undergo this operation not only will usually completely recover and become seizure free, but will actually gain IQ. points with the removal of the overactive brain cells! I documented the phenomenon of the physical healing process, and inspired a medical research program to help patients and their physicians understand what to expect, post surgery, as the brain reorganizes. I found that providing the patients and their doctors with this information increases understanding of the healing process and diminishes the fears of the patients considerably, which aids them during recovery from this traumatic procedure. I now have the privilege of helping people all over the country. One person who lives in Houston, Texas, wrote me this note after his surgery.

Dear Teri,

I just wanted you to know that I wouldn't be alive right now writing this letter if you hadn't help me prepare for the surgery and the recovery process. I felt so alone. The doctors couldn't help me in this area because they hadn't been there. They could only heal the body. You helped to heal my soul. Thank you for caring enough to share your experience and to help me in mine. You will forever be in my heart and prayers because you literally saved my life. If you hadn't explained some of what I would go through I would have thought something was wrong and I would have shot myself that day.

Greg Nelson

While I was reading his words of thanksgiving, I could hear the inaudible whisper of *"I still care,"* for in his letter, I saw a glimpse of the good that transcends the absurdities of living in a world of undeserved suffering and pain. Wounds are healed by wounds. Scars are healed by scars. I could offer him something no one else could because I had been where he was and I knew his pain. I had lived it. In the realization that I had helped another human being recover from a personal holocaust experience directly because of my own pain, I saw a glimpse of the goodness of God.

Creating good out of senseless suffering includes identification with the inner person, broken humanity to broken humanity. To arrive at intimacy and oneness is to feel the pain of others, "to have the sense of being so 'mixed in' with the mass of suffering humanity that one cannot consider oneself as a distinct or separate being."[78]

To be one with Christ is to be a servant to humanity. To be a servant, to love someone with unconditional love, to bear his burden, is to become as tired as he is.

I know what it is to feel hungry. I will feed you. I know what it is to be thirsty. I will find you a cup of cold water. I know what it is to be in tremendously agonizing pain. I will help you find relief. I will cry with you. My inner person cries for your inner person. I will walk beside you, my friend.

I am using the theological term "inner person" to represent what goes on inside of all of us. The "outer person" is what others see and the image we portray to other people. The "inner person" and the "outer person" can be worlds apart. The "outer person" can appear to the outside world as being brave, happy, having "it" all together while the "inner person" cries silently, feeling insecure at times, lonely, afraid, and unsure. Part of finding purpose for your pain is in discovering that what you have experienced inside of you, those thoughts of uncertainty about organized religion — the outer person says *"Amen"* while the inner person says *"I don't quite buy that!"* — the aloneness of despair, the God-forsakenness you've experienced, the reality of the Nothing answering when you pray, the fear of the future, the disappointment of the past, are the same experiences in the "inner person" of all humanity. We stoic Christians are good at putting on a together "outer person" front. Yet, the work of God will not result from this egotism from which we all suffer, but will result when we have an attitude of humility. Why? Because the Bible tells us that humility is wisdom and good deeds come from it.

"Who is wise and understanding among you? Let him show it by his good life, by deeds done in the humility that comes from wisdom."
(James 3:13, NIV)

Humility usually is a product of a personal humiliation experience, an experience when we realize we are not really in control of our lives and we begin to look outside of ourselves for answers and strength. When we acknowledge our weaknesses, we gain true strength and then God can use us to make sense out of what seems senseless and will help us create a purpose for what seems purposeless.

How can you create a purpose? By realizing that what you have experienced that has brought pain into your life can help you identify with someone else's "inner person." By using your experience to help another person who is hurting, you are helping God create something powerful from what seems to be the weakest area of your life.

"My grace is sufficient for you, for power is made perfect in weakness. So, I will boast all the more gladly of my weaknesses, so that the power of Christ may dwell in me. Therefore I am content with weaknesses, insults, hardships, persecutions, and calamities for the sake of Christ; for whenever I am weak, then I am strong.
(2 Cor. 12:9-10, NRSV)

When we use the unfortunate things that have happened to us to help another person, the great renovator of civic centers can turn our lives into one concert hall where the symphony always plays.

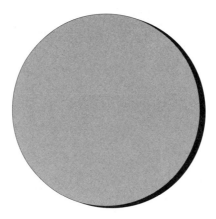

Another analogy would be to turn the cross that you have had to bear in life into a bridge for another. In doing this you follow the path of Christ when He said, *"Take up your cross and follow me."* (Mark 8:34)

What is He saying to us? I believe He is reminding us first and foremost that we will all have crosses to bear. It is just a fact of life in this world we live in. Bad things do happen to good people through no fault whatsoever of their own. The theology of the exceptionalistic, sometimes charismatic religion that people get sick and are not healed because of sin in their lives or because of a lack of faith is simply a denial of the results of living in an imperfect world and a denial of death. If anyone ever tells you anything similar, simply smile and say *"I thought God took care of Job's friends a long time ago. I guess some people haven't caught on yet!"*

Please understand that those who must endure physical afflictions, disappointments, pain, and suffering in any area of life, and who are praying and believing, but are not seeing immediate answers to their prayers, are living the faith journey and their walk is to be respected. You are living the faith journey or you wouldn't be searching to create a purpose for the unjust pain you've endured. I respect your journey. By enduring, you are picking up the cross of Jesus and carrying on His message. We all have crosses to bear. The important thing is what you decide to do with that cross. Jesus used His cross to give the world eternal life. You can use yours to build a bridge for another suffering soul with whom you can identify inner person to inner person.

You have been damaged. But you have great hope. The mercy of God does not eradicate the damage, at least not in this life, but it soothes the soul and draws it forward to a hope that purifies and sets free. Allow the pain of the past and the travail of the change process to create fresh new life in you and to serve as a bridge which another victim may walk from death to life.

Dan Allender

161

THE CHASM

A chasm loomed before me,
A chasm deep and wide.
I stood trembling on the brink,
And viewed the other side.

My heart was filled with terror.
My body groaned in pain.
My broken spirit dared not hope,
That I'd be well again.

"It's all so dark," I cried in fear,
as waters raged below.
The Nothing screamed, yet,
God was near,
as time would gently show.

I said a tiny thread of prayer,
with a little more than hope.
The first of countless other prayers,
that at last became a rope.

At last a bridge of faith was built
from anguish and despair,
through the many times
I questioned God,
"Do you even care?"

Now that I have safely passed
All the anguish left behind,
A million other sufferers
Come marching through my mind.

Had I not crossed this bridge of faith,
not built for me alone,
A glimpse of God could have been
missed,
might never have been know.

A glimpse of God can be found
in spite of all the loss,
God spanned the chasm of man's need
With Calvary's rugged cross.

And so my "cross" may be a bridge,
for another who is in pain,
So he can say *"in spite of it all,
I can believe again."*

—Maurice Berquist/Teri Messner

Part of building that bridge includes being able to thank God for nothing.[79] I chose to do just that by writing the following letter.

Letter to God

Dear God,

THANKS FOR NOTHING. My dreams, one by one, have been stripped away. I remember so vividly living in pleasant, passive oblivion, believing that as long as I did not see the pain in the world, it did not exist. Believing that if it truly did, I was exempt. In my pious Christianity, believing that I would be granted blessings abundant from God because I called Him my God. Believing, somehow, I was chosen to be sheltered, to be pampered, destined for greatness to proclaim God's kingdom.

I prayed for wisdom.
I received pain.

I prayed for happiness.
I received desperation.

I prayed for health.
I received affliction.

I prayed for friends.
I was abandoned.

Because I received nothing,
I experienced pain.

Because I received nothing,
I experienced humiliation.

Because I received nothing,
My eyes were opened to
    others who have nothing.

I can embrace those who have
    nothing,
Because I have cried their cry.

Thanks for nothing,
For it's because of that gift that I have received everything.

"Blessed are the poor in spirit, for theirs is the kingdom of Heaven.
Blessed are those who mourn, for they shall be comforted.
Blessed are the gentle, for they shall inherit the earth.
Blessed are those who hunger and thirst for righteousness,
for they shall be satisfied.
Blessed are the merciful, for they shall receive mercy.
Blessed are the pure in heart, for they shall see God.
Blessed are the peace makers, for they shall be called the Sons of God.
Blessed are those who have been persecuted for the sake of righteousness,
for theirs is the kingdom of heaven.
Blessed are you when men cast insults at you and persecute you and say
all kinds of evils against you falsely on account of me. Rejoice and be
glad, for your reward in heaven is great, for so they persecuted the
prophets who were before you."

(Matt. 5: 1-11, NAS)

Why thank God for nothing? In my short lifetime, I have experienced the extremes that life can give. I have been a beauty queen, a singer, and a television show host who signed autographs and received applause. Almost overnight, I became one of the "less thans" of society, having to endure a misunderstood illness, and then as a hospital patient I was treated as less than human by a few arrogant physicians. At first glance, the previously glamorous part of my life seems to be the time of blessing, but since I have recovered from the latter part, I have realized that it was the painful years that helped me to understand what is going on in the "inner person" of hurting humanity, largely because I chose to create a purpose for the meaningless pain that I suffered so that another hurting soul may be able to see a glimpse of God.[80] How can a beauty queen help humanity? How can a beauty queen who has never truly experienced hardship understand what is going on in the "inner person" of people who have? It was through the pain in my

164

life that I can now identify with broken humanity.[81] It was through the pain that Jesus suffered as a man who lived on the earth that enabled God to identify with His creation. I believe He chose the path of suffering because He was trying to tell us to always look at the world in an upside-down fashion, for God will one day turn this upside-down world right-side up and those who have faithfully endured will receive a just reward.

It was through my personal journey of pain, not through my moments of glamour, that I learned to identify with all people who have been broken by life and through this identification, found something meaningful. It has been because of my scars that I have earned the privilege to help heal yours. When we use the scars that life has left us with to help someone else get through and recover from their battles in life, we are mirroring Christ's example when He showed His nail-pierced hands and wounded side to His disciple Thomas.

So the other disciples told him, "We have seen the Lord." But he
said to them, "Unless I see the mark of the nails in his hands,
and put my finger in the mark of the nails
and my hand in his side, I will not believe."
A week later his disciples were again in the house,
and Thomas was with them. Although the doors were shut,
Jesus came and stood among them and said,
"Peace be with you."
Then he said to Thomas, "Put your finger here and see my hands.
Reach out your hand and put it in my side.
Do not doubt but believe.

(John 20: 25-27, NRSV)

A few months after I had recovered from surgery, I was given my first opportunity to use my scar to help someone heal. I was told of a little girl who was facing the same surgery that I had undergone. She was in a local hospital undergoing final testing before being sent out of town for the first brain surgery. I thought to myself, *"I know she's got to be frightened. Maybe she'd like to talk with someone who has survived it."* I wanted to meet her.

I walked into the hospital room and found a lovely twelve-year-old girl with beautiful dark eyes and strikingly thick, naturally curly, long brown hair.

"You must be Ashly." I said.

"Yes, ma'am, but who are you? You don't look like a nurse. You don't have white on," she sweetly observed.

"No dear. I'm the lady your doctor told you about who has had the same surgeries you're going to have."

"But you have hair!" she exclaimed. "You have long hair! How long ago did you have the surgery?"

"Just a few weeks ago."

"But don't they have to shave your head?" She asked with surprise.

"No dear, the more advanced doctors don't require that anymore."

"You mean I get to keep my hair? Wow!" She seemed relieved. "Where's the scar? Is it terrible?"

As I lifted up my bangs to uncover the thin, barely visible scar that runs across the top of my head, I thought, *"My scar will help her prepare for hers and will help calm her fear."* Without a scar, I couldn't have helped her. At that moment I was thankful that I wear a battle wound from the war of life. It has been worth it all to help relieve the fears of one small child. I had already begun to use the senseless pain that had randomly entered into my life to help another person who was hurting.

"That's all there is?" She asked.

"Yes, that's all there is." Her lovely eyes began to fill with threatening tears.

"I'm so scared." She whispered. "Will I be okay? Does it hurt?"

"I know you're scared. I was scared, too. That's why I came to see you. I wanted you to know that you're going to be all right. I won't lie to you, Ashly. It does hurt, but only for a little while and then it will be all over and you'll be better than okay. You'll never have to have those silly seizures again. You'll love that, won't you?"

We talked for a while longer. As I was leaving she reached up to hug me and whispered, "Thank you for being my friend. I'm not as scared now."

"You're not alone, sweetheart. I'll always be your friend. You're going to be okay. I've been there. I know. I made it through and you will too." As I walked out of her room, I felt the most fulfilled I had ever felt in my life. I realized that if I had not experienced the fear, I would not have been able to help calm hers. "Thanks, God, for a glimpse of your goodness in spite of the hard times." I whispered.

As I was about to leave her floor, I saw a man alone in his hospital room, lying on his bed with electrodes attached to his chest. His brow was wrinkled in pain. I noticed that there weren't any flowers or cards decorating the cold room. He looked so alone. His eyes brightened as I peered into the room. I decided this was an invitation. "Do you need a friend?" I asked. He nodded affirmatively.

As I sat with him, I learned that he was a seventy-four-year-old widower who had just suffered his second stroke. He couldn't move most of his body and was in tremendous pain.

"I'm so thirsty." He whispered.

I took a sponge from his bedside tray and dipped it in water to moisten his lips. I mentally recalled a moment, just a few weeks previously, when I had been the patient.

In my mind, I could visualize lying on the hospital bed the day after surgery, with thirty-seven staples in my head, blood-filled hair, and swollen black eyes. I remembered a hospital volunteer who had peeked into my room to see if I was in need of anything. I told her, *"Just water."*

She walked in, lifted my head in her arms, and helped me take a sip of water. I remembered the pain. I remembered how her presence at that time was more comforting than the sip of water was refreshing. I remembered how scared I was. I remembered how alone I felt. I remembered …

Then I looked down into the gentleman's eyes and realized that I understood where he was. I could see the intense pain, the aloneness, and the fear in his eyes, and I understood part of what he was feeling although I didn't even know his name. His eyes echoed what I had experienced. He asked me to *"please"* stay with him for *"just a little while;"* so I sat with him for the remainder of the rainy afternoon barely conversing. We just sat and shared his pain. Although our pain had different names, I knew his inner torment. I knew his aloneness. I knew his fear. I had been where he was. We had both experienced the worst of life. We were both acquainted with the Nothing. We had endured much hardship. We had visited our own graves. We had tasted death, and now we were survivors.

As I bent down to kiss his forehead to say "good-bye," I thought to myself, "Maybe I have helped him to see a glimpse of the goodness of God in spite of all the pain. Thank you, God, that I can identify with his pain. Thank you for the privilege of that knowledge. *Thanks for Nothing."*

The Hand that touches is the hand that was pierced.
A pierced hand is tender. It knows the feeling of pain. [82]
Amy Carmichael

What are you thinking right now? Can you thank God for Nothing? Are you getting a glimpse of how you can use your pain to help someone else heal? Do you realize how important you are? Do you understand that you have a gift to give this world that no one else can give? Do you realize that we who have endured and are yet enduring are called blessed? Do you realize that you are the faith-filled believer? Do you believe that God's goodness can transcend even the worst that has happened to you and that a glimpse of God can one day be found in spite of the unjust suffering that has randomly come into your life? Why? How? Because "Power is perfected in weakness." (2 Cor. 12:9) God can work through your deepest hurts to show His enduring, everlasting love.

The weak are mighty when they turn their problems into projects, their sorrows into servants, their difficulties into dividends, their obstacles into opportunities, their tragedies into triumphs, their stumbling blocks into stepping stones. They look upon an interruption as an interesting interlude. They harvest fruit from frustration. They convert enemies into friends. They look at adversities as adventures.

Robert Schuller
The Be Happy Attitudes

We are continuously faced by great opportunities brilliantly disguised as insoluble problems. Create opportunity from your problems. Your life is important. Your pain is important. Your struggles are to be respected. You can create something meaningful from the purposeless pain that you have had to endure.

I encourage you for your own happiness and benefit to allow the pressure of living on this earth to turn your heartaches into diamonds instead of dust. I encourage you to make a difference in this world of ours, which may mean reaching out to just one person to help her see a glimpse of God. I encourage you to reach out and help revive, rejuvenate, and reinvigorate this hurting world and to help the great renovator of civic centers to restore broken lives. I encourage you to persevere when life is tough, to face obstacles with creative courage as you reach for the crown of a fulfilling life.

Remember, my friend, you are already approved. The crown of life that God has promised is not a glittering, empty dream. The crown God is offering isn't made of rhinestones that tarnish in time, but of diamonds that begin from a lump of coal, go through a painful process that includes years of enduring the pressures of living in an imperfect world to be able to reflect the light of the one who wore a crown made of thorns. I encourage you to continue to reach for the crown of life, with the understanding that you are already a champion of faith. The German-Jewish word for "crown" is *keter,* which translates "divine nothing." The concept behind this word is that there is nothing beyond God.[83] In other words, the crown of Nothing contains everything. This aids us in understanding the message of the man who wore a crown of thorns, the Christ of Humiliation, the Christ who recognized that true faith is always found in the endurer rather than in the idealist, the Christ who was well acquainted with the Nothing. Rest in the knowledge that your struggle is respected by those of us who know what it means to suffer. You are a hero of faith.

All these people were still living by faith when they died.
They did not receive the things promised;
they only saw them and welcomed them from a distance.
(Hebrews 11:13, NIV)

170

Notes

Chapter Two: The Fairy Tale Ends

[1]Barth, Karl, *Dogmatics in Outline* (New York: Harper and Row, 1959), p. 20. "When we believe, we must believe in spite of God's hiddenness. This hiddenness of God necessarily reminds us of our human limitations."

[2]Moltmann, Jurgen, *The Crucified God* (San Francisco: Harper Collins, 1991), p. 36. Moltmann quotes Hegel: "Our faith must be born where it is abandoned by all tangible reality: it must be born of nothingness, it must taste this nothingness and be given it to taste in a way that no philosophy of nihilism can imagine."

[3]Altizer, Thomas J. J., *The Altizer-Montgomery Dialogue,* A Chapter in the God is Dead Controversy (Chicago: Inter Varsity Press, 1967), pp. 16, 17. "Every man who now lives in the history following the advent of Christ lives decisively in a time of the death of God. And inescapably, he must live within a reality in which he no longer can know the presence of the transcendent Lord. He must inevitably live in a time of the eclipse of God, or the silence of God, or the absence of God...every man participates in the body of Christ in-so-far as the body of Christ incorporates and embodies the death of God." Although I believe Altizer deals honestly with the problem of the silence of God, it seems that he falls short of trying to understand the possibility of God using Christ as an example of communicating with us through the experience of the Nothing. Christ's abandonment on the cross gives the Christian the courage to believe "in spite of" (Barth) a silent God. Through identification with Christ's humanity we can discover the goodness of God's divinity. Then the Nothing can be accepted as God's way of communicating with us thereby we can experience His presence.

Chapter Three: Serpents and Stones

[4]Wiesel, Elie, *Night* (Bantam: New York, 1982)

[5]Vicchio, Stephen J., *The Voice From The Whirlwind* (Westminster, Md., Christian Classics, Inc. 1989), p. 87.

[6]Vicchio, p. 250. "Only at the cross can an adequate theodicy be constructed."

[7]Translation: Eugene Peterson, *The Message* (Colorado Springs: NavPress, 1993)

[8]Berkhof, Louis, *Christian Doctrine* (Grand Rapids: Eerdmans Publishing, 1991), p. 190 "We are often inclined to think of the sufferings of Christ as limited to His final agonies. Yet, His whole life was a life of sufferings."

[9]Becker, Ernest, *The Denial of Death* (New York: The Free Press, 1973), p. 89. "Self must be brought down to nothing in order to understand the powers beyond." The bringing down of self includes the acceptance that the Creator has the right to be silent about the problem of evil and includes respecting His silence instead of resenting it.

[10]Tillich, Paul, *The Shaking Of The Foundations* (New York: Charles Scribner's Sons, 1976), p. 5. "The greatest triumph of science was the power it gave to man to annihilate himself and his world... In this way science has closed our eyes and thrown us into an abyss of ignorance about the few things that really matter." The false prophets are those who try to establish the kingdom of God on earth by denying the reality of earthly suffering. Largely because of the advancement of science, many think we have a divine right to achieve perfect health and attain prosperity. The cross destroys this theology.

[11]Ryan, William, *Blaming the Victims* (New York: Random House, Vintage Books)

[12]Sine, Tom, *Wild Hope* (Dallas: Word Publishing, 1991), p. 213. "Evangelical Christians, in the main, have not only enthusiastically made the Western Dream their own; they often look at their material success as evidence of God's blessings in their lives."

[13]Sine, p. 95. "The problem with the current vision of the mainline Christians is that it's not Biblical."

[14]Gilkey, Langdon, *Message and Existence* (San Francisco: Harper and Row), p. 189. "Who we really are, what the requirements and possibilities of being really human, and what we should or could be are questioned and debated, answered and unanswered throughout history... In Jesus, for Christians, an answer, a model, a paradigm of authentic humanity has appeared; the possibilities of human existence are here defined and enacted, and thus the requirements of being fully human for the first time are made plain." The requirement of being fully human includes pain, sufferings, and finally death.

[15]Sine, p. 202. "God is in the process of giving birth to a whole new order that will turn this world upside down." What we value as church members and leaders is still largely what the world values. We love success. We love the glamorous. It's time to reevaluate where we are going and what we stand for. According to Christ's teaching the greatest will be the least and the least the greatest. As Christians we should view the world in the opposite order, the up-side down fashion that was taught by Jesus.

[16]Bretall, Robert, (ed.) *A Kierkegaard Anthology* (Princeton: Princeton University Press, 1973), p. 34, Kierkegaard states: "I have lost my illusions." One must lose the illusion of a pain-free existence in order to truly understand the meaning behind the word *faith*.

[17]Barth, p. 20. "Faith is a freedom, a permission that the believer may be permitted to hold on to this word in everything, in spite of all that contradicts it. Faith is a decision once and for all."

[18]Frankl, Viktor E., *The Doctor and the Soul* (New York: Vintage Books, 1986), p. xvi. "Again and again we have seen that an appeal to continue life, to survive the most unfavorable conditions, can be made only when such survival appears to have a meaning."

Chapter Four, Broken Illusions

[19]Gilkey, Langdon, *Message and Existence* (San Francisco: Harper and Row), p. 184. "The proclaimer apparently ended in futility and error. His message of the kingdom and the future thoroughly contradicted by the reality. Only with His resurrection was that message of confidence in God, in God's future and thus, in the reality of the Kingdom justified again, but now re-interpreted through His death and subsequent resurrection...Characterized by two new factors, first, the deeper realization of the estrangement or darkness of the world and second, the realization of the revelatory and redemptive significance of the total event itself of Jesus as the Christ or Lord, or His coming, His life, His death, His resurrection." The cross was crucial because its darkness transcends man's ability to understand that a loving God would allow it. The very fact we can't comprehend it is a testimony to its validity. The paradoxical nature of Christianity is what leads me to take its teaching seriously.

[20]Arayon, Victoria, *God of the Poor; the Mystery of God in Latin American Liberation Theology* (New York: Mary Knoll, Orbis, 1981), p. 31.

[21]Bretall, p. xxii, " When Christianity is made so attractive that pretty nearly everyone accepts it as a matter of course, then one can be sure it is not true Christianity that is being presented—not the Christianity of Him who made the taking up of one's cross the condition of discipleship."

[22]Bretall, p. 4. A quote from Kierkegaard's journals: "admonishing that the fortunate person is the one to whom the two mighty forces of pride and humility unite together in marriage."

[23]Wisdom, John, "Paradox and Discovery," in *Paradox and Discovery* (Oxford: Oxford University Press, 1965), p. 124. "...though some statements which seem contradictory are self-contradictory, others are not, indeed some of the most preposterous statements ever made have turned out to convey the most important discoveries."

[24]Altizer, p. 13. "The Death of God theology is attempting to say that the fullness, the totality of God Himself is embodied, is made flesh, in Christ is itself emptied of its preincarnate power and glory by the process of its becoming incarnate in Christ."

[25]Sanders, J. Oswald, *Spiritual Leadership* (Chicago: Moody Press, 1967), "Jesus voluntarily emptied Himself, (Phil. 2:7) surrendering His privileges and the independent exercise of His Will."

[26]Vicchio, p. 223, 230. Analysis of the paradox of the fully human, fully divine, Christ.

[27]Vicchio, p. 225. "In the same way that a skilled cricket batsman could choose to play a match from his weaker side of the wicket, so too an omnipotent being could choose to temporarily limit his power so he might truly become human. An omniscient being could choose not to know the truth of certain propositions or a whole range of propositions for that matter." God's omniscience is displayed in His willful limitations. The Kenotic incarnation is the foundation of my proposed theology.

[28]*The Jerusalem Bible* (London: Darton, Longman and Todd, 1968).

[29]Kettler, Christian D., *The Vicarious Humanity of Christ and the Reality of Salvation* (Lanham, Maryland: University Press of America, 1991.)

[30]Altizer, p. 10, 11. "We're attempting to understand God, the God who as Lord—transcendent Lord and Creator—becomes flesh, undergoing a transformation, a process of self-negation or self-annihilation. He negates Himself as transcendent Lord so that He may pass into flesh, so that He may become flesh, so that He may indeed become embodied in concrete time and space... To confess that God has died in Christ is to believe that God Himself has truly, actually, finally and completely entered the world in Christ; that He has fully become embodied in time and space in Christ; that He has emptied Himself, of His own original plenitude. Therein He darkens and empties a transcendent realm, and releases the fullness of His own life and power into the world as a source of life and redemption so that finally, as Paul says, God may become all in all. So, to confess the death of God is simply a means of confessing the life, and indeed the redemptive life, of Jesus Christ."

[31]Schopenhauer, Arthur, *The Pessimists Handbook* (Lincoln: University of Nebraska Press, 1964), "It is absurd to look upon the enormous amount of pain that abounds everywhere in the world, originates in needs and necessities, inseparable from life itself, as serving no purpose at all and the result of mere chance."

[32]Becker, Ernest, Commentary on "The Pawnbroker," 1967.

[33]Vicchio, p. 105.

[34]Vicchio, p.105. "It is self-contradictory to say that a creator, at least in the religions of paradox, is not responsible in some sense for the origin of evil."

[35]Moltmann, p. x. "Whatever can stand before the face of the Crucified Christ is true Christian theology."

[36]Frankl, p. xix "The right kind of suffering, facing your fate without flinching is the highest achievement that has been granted to man."

[37]Gilkey, p. 177.

[38]Vicchio, Chapter III, Analysis of Traditional Theodicies. (I am not endorsing greater good theodicy that evil in some way brings about a good for ultimate future harmony, or the "necessity of evil" theodicy, but I am acknowledging that suffering is a reality of living in the temporal world and historically was used by God in spite of evil for a good and thereby points to a mystery of possible meaningful suffering.)

[39]Hick, John, *Evil and the God of Love* (San Francisco: Harper and Row, 1987), "We ought to reject the traditional theories that would rationalize the incidence of misery: the theory that each individual's sufferings represent a just punishment for his own sins and the theory that the world is in the grip of evil powers, so that the dysteleological surplus of human misery is an achievement of demonic malevolence. Moreover, I do not have an alternative theory to offer that would explain in any rational way why men suffer as they do. The only appeal left is to mystery."

[40]Kettler, Christian D. *Church History, Faith and Reason Lectures,* (Wichita, KS, Friends University, 1992, 1993.) The bases for the faith to live in spite of disappointments are the combination of the theology of the cross and the theology of glory. Temporal pain can be transcended by the hope of eternal glory as revealed in Christ. Because of the life, sufferings, God-forsakenness and death of Jesus, we have been given the hope to believe that ultimately God's goodness will transcend all of life's agony and triumph in the resurrection.

[41]Moltmann, p. 5.

[42]Becker, Ernest, *The Denial Of Death* (New York: The Free Press, 1973), p. 91. "Man breaks through the bounds of merely cultural heroism; he destroys the character lie that had him perform as a hero in the everyday social scheme of things; and by doing so he opens himself up to infinity, to the possibility of cosmic heroism, to the very service of God. His life thereby acquires ultimate values in place of merely social and cultural, historical value. He links his secret inner self, his authentic talent, his deepest feelings of uniqueness, his inner yearning for absolute significance, to the very ground of being."

Chapter Five: Why Me? Why You?

[43]Vicchio, p. 253. My personal teleological response to "all things working together for the good," isn't based on a shallow optimism about world history, but is grounded in the saving work of Jesus Christ in the context of the cross.

Chapter Six: Blaming The Victims

[44]*Strong's Exhaustive Concordance,* Bible Copyright 1986, Word Publishing Inc.

[45]Hanegraaff, Hank, *Christianity In Crisis,* Harvard House, 1993, Audio track.

[46]Hanegraaff, Audio track.

[47]Kettler, Christian, *Faith and Reason Lectures,* (Friends University, Wichita, KS, Spring 1993) The Problem of Fundamentalism: tendency to ignore the connection between "lalia" and "logos." Correct interpretation of scripture must include a Unitary Knowledge combining the "lalia" and the "logos."

[48]Hanegraaff, Audio track.

[49]Anderson, Ray S., *Theological Foundations for Ministry* (Pasadena: Anderson, 1989), p. 316.

[50]Sine, Tom, *Wild Hope* (Dallas: Word Publishing, 1991), p.187. "I am concerned that these groups (Charismatics and Pentecostals) haven't done their homework."

[51]Barth, p. 11. "Christian Dogmatics will always be a thinking, an investigation and an exposition which are relative and liable to error. Even Dogmatics with the best knowledge and the best conscience can do no more than question after the better."

[52]Sine, p. 224. "God's purposes include to turn the world upside down— pulling down the rich and the powerful and lifting up the poor and the marginalized."

[53]Anderson, pp. 580, 581, 582. Anderson speaks for solidarity with Christ (solidarity meaning unity of purpose).

[54]Anderson, p. 577.

[55]Vicchio, p. 231. The kenotic twist enables one to take the pain of the individual sufferer seriously while it responds to the problem of evil.

[56]Hanegraaff, Audio track.

[57]Kettler, p. 98. "Unity is not a prison, but a freedom..." God was unified with humanity through the life and death of Christ. We are unified with Christ through the taking up of our own cross. *"He who does not take his cross and follow after Me is not worthy of Me."* (Matt. 10: 38)

Chapter Seven: The Garden

[58]Beausobre, Iulia De, *Creative Suffering* (Oxford: SLG Press, 1984.) We should be inspired, "with a firm resolve to refuse the temptation to seek any more superficial solutions to the most pressing of our difficulties."

[59]Smail, *The Forgotten Father,* p. 43.

[60]Frankl, p. 116. "I want to clarify that although the good doctor is there to help, he/she is not the hero. The patient is. The patient, as the sufferer, is superior to the doctor... A doctor who is sensitive to the imponderables of a situation will always feels a kind of shame when attending a patient with an incurable disease, or a dying person...But the patient has become a hero who is meeting his fate and holding his own, accepting it in tranquil suffering."

[61]Anderson, p. 311.

[62]Sider, Ronald J., *Evangelism, Salvation, and Social Justice*, (Grove Books.)

[63]Sine, p. 134. "A mother of an infant born in a Palestinian village many years ago reminds us of God's intention to turn the world right side up."

And His mercy is on those who fear Him from generation to generation, He has shown strength with His arm. He has scattered the proud in the imagination of their hearts. He had put down the mighty from their thrones, and exalted those of low degree; He has filled the hungry with good things,
and the rich he has sent away empty. (Luke 1: 50-53, RSV)

Chapter Nine: Graveside Reflections

[64]Bonhoeffer, Dietrich, *Letters and Papers From Prison* (New York: Macmillan Publishing Company, 1971), p. 326. "Absolute seriousness is never without a dash of humor."

[65]Neary, Donal, *The Calm Beneath the Storm* (Chicago: Loyola University Press, 1983.)

Chapter Ten: Faith: Facing Reality With Eagle Courage

[66]Becker, p. 92. "...as long as man is an ambiguous creature he can never banish anxiety; what he can do instead is to use anxiety as an eternal spring for growth into new dimensions of thought and trust. Faith poses a new life task, the adventure in openness to a multidimensional reality."

[67]Bonhoeffer, p.376. "Death is the supreme festival on the road to freedom."

[68]Barth, p. 19 "...faith involves in spite of" The bases for faith are the combination of the theology of the cross and the theology of glory. Temporal pain can be transcended by the hope of eternal glory as revealed in Christ. Because of the life, sufferings, God-forsakenness and death of Jesus, we have been given the hope to believe that ultimately God's goodness will transcend all of life's agony and triumph in the resurrection.

[69]Becker, p. 257. Becker explains Kierkegaard's "Knight of faith" as the figure of a man who lives in faith, who has given over the meaning of life to his Creator, and who lives centered on the energies of his Maker. He accepts whatever happens in this visible dimension without complaint, lives his life as a duty, faces his death without a qualm.

[70]Bretall, p. 118. Bretall quotes Kierkegaard discussing the "Knight of Faith." Kierkegaard analyzes the fact that we humans never can seem to stop with faith, we always want to go further. But ultimately that is all there is.

[71]Luther, Martin, *Three Treatises* (Fortress Press, 1970), pp. 18,27.

[72]Bonhoeffer, p. 382. "The church is only the church when it exists for others."

[73]Becker, p. 158. Becker writes of Kierkegaard's "immediate" men and the "Philistines" who tranquilize themselves with the trivial so that they can lead normal lives.

Chapter Eleven: Now What? Victim or Victor

[74]Storms, Randy, *Between the Lighting and the Thunder* (Eugene, Oregon: Harvest House Publishers, 1989.)

[75]Kavanaugh, James, *There are Men Too Gentle to Live Among Wolves* (New York: Sunrise Books, 1970.)

[76]Lauren A. King's *"Dressed For The Struggle."*

Chapter Twelve: Your Cross—A Bridge, Your Life— A Symphony

[77]Moltmann, p. 46.

[78]Woolman, John, *The Journal of John Woolman and A Plea for the Poor* (Philadelphia: Citadel Press, Corinth Books, 1961), p. X.

[79]Altizer, p.17 "Now I believe that the Christian can rejoice in the death of God. He can rejoice in the loss of transcendence. He can even rejoice in the new chaos, the new darkness into which we have been hurled or thrown by our own destiny. He can rejoice because in a certain sense he can know this chaos as the consummation of God's original movement in Christ."

[80]Sanders, "They want a ministry more rewarding and more worthy of their powers— something more spectacular than bearing with the relapses and backslidings of frail humanity; but it is a noble work to reclaim those whom the world despises."

[81]Bonhoeffer, p. 17. I have learned to see the world from below, "...from the perspective of the outcast, the suspects, the maltreated, the powerless, the oppressed, the reviled—in short, from the perspective of those who suffer."

[82]Elliot, Elisabeth, *A Chance To Die, The Life and Legacy of Amy Carmichael* (New York: Fleming H. Revell Company, 1987.)

[83]Palnik, Paul. *Author of Eternaloons (*Columbus, Creative Light Press, 1991.)

References

Altizer, Thomas J. J. *The Altizer-Montgomery Dialogue, A Chapter in the God is Dead Controversy.* Chicago: Inter -Varsity Press, 1967.

Anderson, Ray S. *Theological Foundations For Ministry.* Pasadena: Anderson, 1989.

Arayon, Victoria. *God of the Poor; The Mystery of God in Latin American Liberation Theology.* New York: Mary Knoll, Orbis, 1981.

Barth, Karl. *Dogmatics in Outline.* New York, Harper and Row, 1959.

Beausobre, Iulia De. *Creative Suffering.* Oxford: SLG Press, 1984.

Becker, Ernest. *The Denial of Death.* New York: The Free Press, 1973.

Becker, Ernest. Commentary on "The Pawnbroker," 1967.

Berkhof, Louis. *Christian Doctrine.* Grand Rapids: Eerdmans Publishing, 1991.

Boff, Leonardo, Clodovis. *Introducing Liberation Theology.* New York: Orbis, 1989.

Bonhoeffer, Dietrich. *Letters and Papers From Prison.* New York: Macmillan Publishing Company, 1971.

Bretall, Robert, ed. *A Kierkegaard Anthology.* Princeton: Princeton University Press, 1973.

Elliot, Elizabeth. *A Chance To Die, The Life and Legacy of Amy Carmichael.* New York: Fleming H. Revell Company, 1987.

Frankl, Viktor E. *The Doctor and the Soul.* New York: Vintage Books,1986.

Gilkey, Langdon. *Message and Existence.* San Francisco: Harper and Row.

Hanegraaff, Hank. *Christianity In Crisis.* Harvard House, 1993. Audio Tapes.

Hick, John. *Evil and the God of Love.* San Francisco: Harper and Row, 1987.

The Jerusalem Bible. London: Darton, Longman and Todd, 1968.

Kettler, Christian D. *The Vicarious Humanity of Christ and the Reality of Salvation.* Lanham, NY, London: University Press of America, 1991.

Kettler, Christian D. Lectures, Friends University, 1992-1993: Faith and Reason, Church History, Theology of Ministry.

Luther, Martin. *Three Treatise.* Fortress Press, 1970.

Moltmann, Jurgen. *The Crucified God.* San Francisco: Harper Collins, 1991.

Ryan, William. *Blaming the Victims.* New York: Random House, Vintage Books.

Sanders, J. Oswald. *Spiritual Leadership*. Chicago: Moody Press, 1967.

Schmemann, Alexander. *For the Life of the World*. Crestwood, NY: St. Vladimir's Seminary Press, 1988.

Schopenhauer, Arthur. *The Pessimist's Handbook*. Lincoln: University Press, 1964.

Sider, Ronald. J. *Evangelism, Salvation, and Social Justice*. Grove Books.

Sine, Tom. *Wild Hope*. Dallas: Word Publishing, 1991.

Smail, Thomas. *The Forgotten Father*. Grand Rapids: Grand Rapids Publishing, 1980.

Storms, Randy. *Between the Lighting and the Thunder*. Eugene Oregon: Harvest House Publishers, 1989.

Strong's Exhaustive Concordance, Hebrew and Greek Bible, Copyright 1980, 1986, Dallas: Word Publishing Inc.

Tillich, Paul. *The Shaking of the Foundations*. New York: Charles Scribner's Sons, 1976, p. 5.

Vicchio, Stephen J. *The Voice From The Whirlwind*. Westminster, Md.: Christian Classics, Inc., 1989.

Woolman, John. *The Journal of John Woolman and A Plea for the Poor*. Philadelphia: Citadel Press, Corinth Books, 1961.

To Request Teri Messner for your Speaking Engagement

Contact: CLASS SPEAKERS, INC.
Christian Leaders, Authors & Speakers Services
1645 S. Rancho Santa Fe Road, SUITE 102
San Marcos, CA 92069
1-800-252-7771   (619) 471-1722
FAX (619) 471-8896

Order Form

☎ **Telephone orders:** Call Toll Free: 1(800) 763-9946. Have your Discover, Visa, or Mastercard ready.

✳ **Fax orders:** (316) 729-0584

✉ **Postal Orders:** Wild Wings Inc.
⠀⠀⠀⠀⠀⠀⠀⠀⠀⠀⠀⠀⠀⠀⠀New Wings Division
⠀⠀⠀⠀⠀⠀⠀⠀⠀⠀⠀⠀⠀⠀⠀211 N. 135 W.
⠀⠀⠀⠀⠀⠀⠀⠀⠀⠀⠀⠀⠀⠀⠀Wichita, KS 67235 USA

☐ Please send a brochure of New Wings FREE

Reaching For The Crown — $19.95

Sales tax:
Please add 5.9% for books shipped to Kansas addresses

Shipping:
Book Rate: $2.00 for book and 75 cents for each additional item.
(surface shippping may take three to four weeks)
Air Mail: $3.50 per book

Payment:
☐ Check
☐ Credit card: ☐ Visa ☐ Mastercard ☐ Discover

Card number: _____ Exp. date: ___ /___

Name on card:_____

Call toll free and order now